CW00584744

SCOTT OF TH
ANTARCTIC
AND CARDIFF

ANTHONY M. JOHNSON

With a Foreword by Sir Peter Scott

THE CAPTAIN SCOTT SOCIETY
CARDIFF

First published in 1984 in Great Britain by
University College Cardiff Press
Second Revised Impression 1990

New Edition 1995
Published by The Captain Scott Society
c/o Royal Hotel
St Mary Street
Cardiff CF1 1LL

British Library Cataloguing in Publication Data
Johnson, Anthony M.
  Scott of the Antarctic and Cardiff.
  1. British Antarctic Expedition. 1910—
  Finance.   2. Corporations—Wales—
  Cardiff (South Glamorgan)
  I. Title
  919.8'904   G850.1910.B7

  ISBN 0 9516819 2 3

Printed in Great Britain by
McLays, Cardiff

Contents

Acknowledgements

Permission has been granted by the Council of the Glamorgan History Society to reproduce material which appeared in the Journal of the Society, *Morgannwg*, Vols. XXVI (1982) and XXVII (1983).

Foreword

This monograph makes a welcome addition to our knowledge of Capt. Scott's second Antarctic Expedition—the British Antarctic Expedition (1910). For the first time due attention has been accorded to the role of Cardiff in the fortunes of the Expedition. The Cardiff Docksmen provided support for the enterprise on a scale quite unmatched by any town or group.

In this well researched study it is suggested that without the support which derived from Cardiff the Expedition would not have sailed, let alone have achieved the fame and fascination which its tragic ending continues to arouse. In recognition of Cardiff's special contribution to the Expedition Capt. Scott designated Cardiff as the port to which the *Terra Nova* would return at the end of her voyage.

Throughout the course of a careful examination of the unique connection between Cardiff and the British Antarctic Expedition (1910) there emerges much valuable information about the Docks and Civic communities in Cardiff in the early 1900s.

Peter Scott

The Royal Hotel, St. Mary Street, Cardiff, where, in the Alexandra Room on the evening of Monday 13th June 1910, the Cardiff Chamber of Commerce entertained Capt. Scott and officers of the British Antarctic Expedition (1910) to a farewell dinner.

(Photo Circia 1910 by kind permission of South Glamorgan County Library, Cardiff)

I
The Cardiff connexion established

Both the memoirs of participants in the ill-fated Scott Expedition to
the South Pole—known officially as the British Antarctic Expedition
(1910)—and the succession of accounts of the enterprise published
over the past eighty years have paid scant attention to the role of
Cardiff in the affair beyond recording the fact that the Expedition
departed the United Kingdom from the city aboard the *Terra Nova*
on 15 June 1910. Even the most recent, most exhaustive, and certainly the most controversial study of Scott pays no regard to the
crucial role played by Cardiff in support of the enterprise.[1]

On the face of things Cardiff was an unusual choice as the port of
departure for it was not a place traditionally associated with voyages
of exploration and discovery and certainly no previous expedition
had used Cardiff as its base port. Indeed, the Cardiff connexion with
the Scott Expedition was largely fortuitous. Once, however, the
opportunity to play a central role in the Expedition had presented
itself, over the months of preparation there developed a close commitment by the leading citizens of Cardiff to ensure its success such
that the business community invested money and resources to an
extent quite unmatched by any other town or group of backers in the
United Kingdom. So important were their efforts it can be argued
that without Cardiff's support the Scott Expedition might never
have left Britain on time, let alone have achieved the fame and fascination which its tragic failure continues to arouse.

The genesis of the Cardiff connexion with the Scott Expedition
derived from an attempt by the man who became Scott's second-in-
command, Lt. E.R.G.R. Evans, Evans of 'the Broke', later Admiral
Lord Mountevans, to organise his own expedition to the Antarctic,
independent of, and quite unknown, to Scott.

Evans's enthusiasm for polar exploration had been fuelled by his
experiences as commander of two relief expeditions to the Antarctic
in the second of which he rescued Scott and his companions when in
difficulties in the course of the National Antarctic Expedition of
1901–4—the *Discovery* Expedition. Evans returned from this relief
operation determined that one day he would lead his own expedition

1

to the Antarctic. By the summer of 1909 Evans had drawn up careful
navigational plans in respect of a scheme which he had formulated
for making a quick dash for the South Pole from a base on King
Edward VII Land, which had been sighted but not explored, during
the course of Scott's National Antarctic Expedition of 1901–4.

At some point in the early summer of 1909[2], Evans informed Sir
Clements Markham—a very influential former President of the
Royal Geographical Society—of his proposals and sought his advice
as to the names of 'really rich men' who might be potential sources of
financial support, one of whom was Lord Strathcona[3]. There is no
evidence, however, that before the end of June 1909 Evans made any
approaches to these men or made any other attempts to canvas for
funds.

In the summer of 1909 the South Pole was very much in the news.
In mid-June Shackleton made a triumphant return from his
Expedition on which he achieved 'furthest South', reaching a point
97 miles from the South Pole. At a dinner on 19 June held to
celebrate Shackleton's return Captain Scott announced that he was
prepared to go in search of the South Pole[4]. Towards the end of that
month, probably on 28 June, Evans approached the office of the
High Commissioner in London, Lord Strathcona, former Chairman
of the Hudson's Bay Company, the owners of Scott's *Discovery* and
likely backer, in the course of which he came into contact with W.L.
Griffiths, the Permanent Secretary to the High Commissioner. It so
happened that Griffiths was born in Bangor, Caernarvonshire, and
while a young man had emigrated to Canada where he became a successful farmer and grain exporter to the United Kingdom in which
capacity, in 1897, he took on the task of Canadian Agent in Wales,
followed in 1903 by his appointment as Permanent Secretary to the
High Commissioner in London[5]. At this meeting Evans appraised
Griffiths of his plans for an Antarctic expedition[6], an encounter
which proved a stroke of good fortune for the young lieutenant who,
from an early age, had formed a strong emotional attachment to
Wales and in particular to Cardiff from where, it seems, his paternal
grandfather had originated.

In the circumstances it is more than likely that Wales, Welsh contacts, and the possibilities of financial backing from the booming city
of Cardiff were widely discussed. Be that as it may, soon after the
meeting Griffiths took the initiative to put through a telephone call
to W.E. Davies, the editor of the *Western Mail* in Cardiff, to suggest
that he went up to London the following day to discuss the matter,

not revealed in the telephone conversation, but which he considered to be of great significance 'both to you and Wales'.

In response to Griffiths's intriguing telephone call Davies travelled to London the following day where in the Permanent Secretary's office at the Canadian High Commission he was given an account of Griffiths's conversation with Evans. As W.E. Davies recalled, Griffiths was in no doubt as to Evans's ultimate aim. 'He is going to the South Pole and it is my belief that anything that young officer undertakes he will carry through. It strikes me that as he is a Welshman— his forbears are from Cardiff—it ought to be possible to make it a Welsh Expedition, and therefore, it is a matter for the *Western Mail*. Anyhow, it seemed to me to be worth your consideration'. That evening, over dinner at the Devonshire Club, Evans unfolded his plans to Davies. It was on this occasion that Davies ventured the possibility of fitting out and promoting an expedition to be led by Evans as an all Welsh enterprise based in Cardiff and it was generally agreed that the prospects for such an enterprise were, on the face of things, good. As editor of the *Western Mail* Davies was an honorary member of the Cardiff Chamber of Commerce[7], and his knowledge of, and close connexions with, the Cardiff business and civic communities were clearly of crucial importance in persuading Evans that Cardiff possessed the resources necessary to promote his enterprise and that its local businessmen would come forward with funds. Indeed, Evans resolved immediately to go ahead and mount an all Welsh Expedition to the South Pole from its base in Cardiff

At the very end of June 1909, probably the day following his discussion with W.E. Davies, Evans called upon Sir Clements Markham to elaborate on his plans for an Antarctic Expedition[8]. The progress which Evans had made in preparing for his own expedition to the southern hemisphere must have come as a distinct surprise to Markham, Scott's mentor and principal supporter over many years, for he came possessed of well thought out plans for an attempt on the Pole supported by extremely good prospects for financing and equipping his Expedition in Cardiff. Markham was left in no doubt that Evans had emerged as a serious rival to Scott to become the first Briton to reach the South Pole. In the circumstances the best Markham could suggest was that Evans should return for luncheon in a week's time for further discussion. On that occasion, 8 July, Markham suggested that Evans should meet with Scott to discuss their respective plans[9] and such a meeting took place a week later on 16 July 1909[10].

It must be assumed that Evans was able to take to his meeting with Scott assurances from W.E. Davies that he would use his influence to encourage the Cardiff business and civic communities to afford full support and facilities for any enterprise which might be agreed between the two men.

We can but speculate at the nature of the discussions between the explorers. Evans would obviously have emphasised the crucial importance of building up the valuable Cardiff connexions which he had recently forged through the good offices of W.E. Davies[11]. He would have pointed out to Scott that the enthusiastic backing of the *Western Mail,* though not a 'national newspaper', would be extremely valuable as a vehicle of publicity in their efforts to secure funds in South Wales. Scott for his part would doubtless have countered Evans's enthusiasm for the Cardiff connexion by drawing attention to the dangers of placing undue reliance on what were, as yet, little more than confident and interested expressions of opinion by the editor of the *Western Mail* that when the Cardiff business and civic communities were asked to throw their support behind the British Antarctic Expedition they would do so with enthusiasm.

Whatever Scott's reservations as to Cardiff's role in his Antarctic enterprise, as a result of this meeting the two men agreed to co-operate rather than compete in their efforts to gain the South Pole. Scott was to assume command of the Expedition and Evans was to be his second-in-command and Captain of the Expedition ship. It seems also that it was decided that Evans should be in the party which made the final assault on the Pole and Scott certainly mentioned this in his Cardiff speeches. This agreement meant that Scott was obliged to discard his promised deputy, Reginald Skelton, already an experienced Polar explorer and skilled engineer.

Even though Scott, probably with prompting from Sir Clements Markham, was ready to accept the value of Evans's Antarctic experience, he had yet to be persuaded to accord Cardiff a prominent role in the Expedition's plans. Immediately W.E. Davies, probably at Evans's behest, met with Scott, and as he later recalled of their discussions, 'Scott did not conceal—indeed he did not attempt to conceal—an impression that Celtic exuberance was responsible for the assurances that Wales would do great things for the Expedition'. Davies himself experienced great difficulty in persuading Scott of the considerable value to the Expedition of forging strong links with Cardiff, and in response to Davies's suggestion that Evans should be detailed to go down to Cardiff to assess for himself just how much support the Expedition was likely to attract there, Scott replied 'I don't want Evans to go down to Cardiff for £25 or so'. Davies was moved to respond that he would not have pursued the matter of Cardiff's support for the proposed Expedition with such vigour if he had not been convinced that it would be forthcoming. And with that, Scott, if not entirely assured of its wisdom even now, was persuaded to allow the Cardiff connexion to proceed[12].

The estimated cost of the British Antarctic Expedition (1910) was put at £50,000. It was hoped that the bulk of this sum, £40,000, would be forthcoming by way of public subscriptions in the United Kingdom while it was confidently anticipated that the remaining £10,000 would be donated by well wishers from the Dominions as the Expedition ship made its way out to its southern headquarters in New Zealand. The high cost of the Expedition—more than twice that of Shackleton's recent 'furthest South' Expedition—is to be explained mainly by the high proportion of Expedition funds which had to be spent on the wages and provisions for a large party of some 65 members, about one-fifth of whom were highly qualified scientists. Though it is said that over 8,000 applications were received for engagement on the Antarctic Expedition, most members were either former colleagues of Scott's from earlier Antarctic ventures—such as Dr. Edward Wilson and P.O. Edgar Evans from Rhosili, near Swansea—or secured their appointments as a result of personal recommendation.

Scott's complement of staff was more than three times larger than the 19 men taken by the Norwegian Roald Amundsen in his historic conquest of the South Pole ahead of Scott. The difference in numbers in itself reflects the attitude and approach of the two explorers to their ambitions in the Antarctic. Whereas Amundsen's only and singular purpose was to claim the South Pole, Scott's Expedition by contrast was designed to combine attainment of the Pole with wider scientific and exploratory work. The personnel of the British Antarctic Expedition (1910) embraced, in effect, two expeditions, the main party under Scott based on McMurdo Sound, and a second party under Lt. Victor Campbell charged with exploratory and scientific work in King Edward VII Land some 400 miles distant[13].

These were, however, distinctions in aim and intent which were largely lost upon an often confused public when they were called upon to subscribe funds for the Scott Expedition, accustomed as they were to rumours of French, Belgian, United States, and even

Japanese preparations for an attack on the Pole. Thus, however much Scott sought during his fund raising campaigns to discourage the notion, there was already in existence in the public's mind 'a race for the Pole' which Britain was expected to win.

There was certainly a race to acquire the requisite funds and to prepare for the Expedition. Scott had under a year to make preparations since it was essential that the British Antarctic Expedition (1910) should depart the United Kingdom not later than August 1910 in order to allow sufficient time for the voyage out to Antarctica and to ensure its establishment of a base camp during the Antarctic summer 1910–11. Failure to meet the departure deadline would have resulted in a delay of another whole year and could well have put paid to Scott's Antarctic ambitions for all time—an eventuality which played constantly on Scott's mind.

The existence of the British Antarctic Expedition (1910) became public knowledge on 13 September 1909 on the occasion of the opening of the Expedition's headquarters at 36 & 38 Victoria Street, London. The *Western Mail* marked the announcement of the proposed Antarctic Expedition with the publication over the next few days of a number of items of news, photographs and maps, which doubtless were designed to persuade people in Cardiff and the surrounding areas of the virtues of the enterprise. From then on the Cardiff based newspaper under the aegis of its editor, W.E. Davies, put the full weight of its authority behind the great venture. Every effort was made to encourage the citizens of Cardiff, and especially the business community, to associate themselves with and to assume a special responsibility for, the success of the Expedition, especially since its second-in-command, the twenty-eight years old Lt. 'Teddy' Evans, had such close links with the city. On 16 September the newspaper quoted Evans—'whose family originally came from Cardiff'—expressing the hope that Wales would afford every support to the Expedition. Later that week, a caption to a photograph of Evans described him as 'a former Cardiff man'[14]. Over the coming months some readers of the *Western Mail* might have been forgiven for thinking that Evans *was* a Cardiff man. In fact Evans's connexions with Cardiff were tenuous. He himself was born in London, while his father, a London barrister, was born in Oldham, Lancashire, the son of a thrice married provision merchant who probably came originally from Cardiff.

The national fund raising campaign, with its target of £40,000, was launched at the Mansion House, London on 12 October, at a contemporary version of the modern day 'Press Conference'. The Lord Mayor of London presided over the meeting flanked by Capt. Scott, Lt. Evans, and other dignitaries, mainly from the Royal Geographical Society, including, significantly, W.E. Davies, the editor of the *Western Mail*. At this meeting there was no mention of the role envisaged for Cardiff in the affairs of the Expedition, though Davies's presence was in itself some indication of the support which it was hoped Cardiff might provide. The next day the *Western Mail* carried a drawing by Lt. Evans of the recently contracted Expedition ship, the *Terra Nova*[15]. Scott had wanted his earlier polar ship, the famous *Discovery*, which he had used on the National Antarctic Expedition of 1901–4, but her owners, the Hudson's Bay Company, were not prepared to make her available on this occasion. Scott settled for the whaler the *Terra Nova* which he contracted to purchase from her owners Bowring Brothers of Liverpool and Newfoundland at an agreed cost of £12,000 though the precise financial arrangements were not finalised until early in November 1909. It was regarded as an acceptable compromise arrangement since both Scott and Evans had experience of the *Terra Nova* in Antarctic waters when she had been employed as a relief ship to the National Antarctic Expedition a few years earlier.

During the months of preparation it was decided that Scott should divide his time between organising the Expedition from its headquarters in London and by going on a succession of fund raising lectures, meetings and dinners, mainly in the Midlands and the North of England. Lt. Evans, naturally, made it his business to concentrate his fund raising activities in Wales and the West of England, which in practice meant Cardiff, as well as over-seeing the preparation and fitting-out of the *Terra Nova* in London.

Within a fortnight of the launching of the national fund raising campaign at the Mansion House, Lt. Evans, together with his New Zealand-born wife, were in Cardiff, as guests on Monday 25 October[16] of the civic authorities, at the ceremonies marking the conferment of the freedom of the city upon Lord Tredegar. Although Lt. Evans, by means of the favourable publicity generated by the *Western Mail*, and privately by W.E. Davies, was becoming a well known figure in Cardiff, this was the first opportunity afforded to him of making personal contact with leaders of the business and civic communities. At this function and over the next few days in a tireless round of lectures and private meetings, with introductions provided by W.E. Davies[17], Lt. Evans canvassed the leading citizens of the city for money and resources for the Antarctic Expedition.

On Saturday, 30 October, Evans delivered in the City Hall his first fund raising lecture—on the Antarctic—much of which, it seems, was devoted to reading out a letter from Sir Clements Markham by means of which Markham endeavoured to persuade the audience that they should see themselves as heirs to a long tradition of Welsh interest in Antarctic exploration which he encouraged them to carry on by lending their support to the Scott expedition. For his efforts Evans received donations totalling £330.5s.0d., one third of which, £105, was donated by the brothers Daniel and Henry Radcliffe. W.E. Davies chose to accompany his newspaper's report of this launching of Evans's fund raising activities in Cardiff with an editorial emphasising the importance of the Expedition which was unashamedly designed to reinforce Evans's appeal for funds[18].

The Monday following, 1 November, Evans was entertained at the Exchange Restaurant in the Docks as the guest of Daniel Radcliffe, J. Herbert Cory and W.C. Tatem (later Lord Glanely). Radcliffe presided at the luncheon at which he explained to the assembled Docksmen that Lt. Evans was anxious to meet the businessmen of the port. Lt. Evans in his reply to Radcliffe's words of support for the Antarctic enterprise, expressed the sentiment that he 'felt perfectly certain that Captain Scott's Expedition would receive the enthusiastic support of the practical businessmen he saw around him'. The young Lieutenant informed his audience that one of their number, Mr. Gethin Lewis,—who on this occasion donated £10.10s.0d.—was the first representative of the Docks community, indeed the first Cardiffian, to have contributed to the funds of the Expedition. In all the sum of £222.17s.0d. was contributed at the luncheon with W.J. Tatem himself donating £100. Mr. Percy Lewis, son of Gethin Lewis, with whom Evans struck up a life-long friendship, was able to announce that Messrs Howell, the Cardiff drapers, had offered to produce for Lt. Evans a large Welsh flag 'to take to the South Pole', a gift which had been provided at the instigation of Mrs. Davies, wife of the editor of the *Western Mail*, who had suggested to Mr. James Howell that his drapery store should provide a Welsh flag[19].

Lt. Evans's speech to the Cardiff Docksmen was characteristic of his approach to fund raising. He always took the view that the best hope of securing support for the Expedition whether in Cardiff or elsewhere, was to play up the commercial advantages of the venture.

And in his address to the Cardiff Docksmen his implicit message was that close association with the Scott Expedition afforded Cardiff—recently elevated to the status of a city—unlimited opportunities for advertisement for its commercial prowess and civic achievements throughout Britain, Europe and even world-wide. He eschewed any attempts to secure financial support built upon an appeal to the benefits of disinterested scientific research favoured by Scott, and as Evans remarked years later, 'We should never have collected our Expedition funds from the Scientific point of view'[20].

While the inspiration behind the Cardiff connexion with the British Antarctic Expedition (1910) was W.E. Davies, outstanding among those who responded to the challenge which it presented and fashioned it into reality, was the leading Cardiff Docksman, Daniel Radcliffe. At this time he was fifty years of age and was, with his elder brother Henry, a partner in the firm of Evan Thomas Radcliffe, ship owners and coal exporters founded by Henry Radcliffe and Evan Thomas. Daniel Radcliffe had joined with his brother as partner in 1892 following the death of Evan Thomas, and contributed much towards the rapid expansion of the company, in the course of which he became one of the most influential and most respected members of the Cardiff Docks community. In 1904 Radcliffe was Chairman of the Cardiff Shipowners Association and by 1910 his company controlled twenty-six vessels to make it the largest ship-owning concern in Cardiff[21].

From their very first meeting in October 1909 Lt. Evans and Daniel Radcliffe struck an immediate rapport with one another which soon developed into a close friendship. Although Radcliffe was quick to appreciate the commercial advantages offered by the Expedition, over the months of preparation for its departure, his interest in the enterprise developed to the extent that his contribution to its success far exceeded self-interested considerations of commercial advantage. He quickly established himself as the driving force behind the fund raising and promotional activities concerning the Antarctic Expedition in Cardiff, and through his friendship with Lt. Evans he assumed the role of unofficial agent and principal coordinator of the interests of the Expedition in the city.

According to local newspapers Evans's first visit to Cardiff had produced the satisfactory total of £545.3s.0d. in subscription money[22]. The deeper significance of his visit, however, was that Evans had consummated the Cardiff connexion with the Scott Expedition by achieving the friendship and confidence of Daniel

Radcliffe and other members of the Docks community, some of the most prominent of whom shared close family as well as business interests, notably Daniel Radcliffe and his brother Henry, W.J. Tatem and Bill Frazer, both brothers-in-law of Daniel Radcliffe. It was a connexion which offered the provision of a wide range of resources, equipment, facilities and technical expertise for the *Terra Nova* and the Expedition, all of which were to ensure that the Expedition departed on time.

After a stay of ten days in Cardiff, Lt. Evans had to return to London on Expedition business, much of which concerned the overseeing of the preparation of the *Terra Nova*, which became the property of the British Antarctic Expedition (1910) early in November 1909 after the arrangements for its purchase had been finalised. The *Terra Nova* was handed over to the Expedition in the West India Dock, London, on 8 November, upon a down payment that day of £5,000, the remainder of which it was agreed by Bowring Brothers should be paid off when the funds of the Expedition allowed[23].

Now Scott was obliged to become a full member of the Royal Yacht Squadron at a cost of £100, a sum which, as Evans said, 'the Expedition could hardly afford'. This was done so that Scott might register the *Terra Nova* as a yacht allowing him to avoid suffering the possible inconvenience and embarrassment of having the ship subject to Board of Trade regulations in respect of crew quarters and overloading[24]; a precaution which proved its worth when the ship faced serious problems arising from overloading when berthed in Cardiff in June 1910, just before its departure for the Antarctic.

Back in Cardiff Daniel Radcliffe and his colleagues built upon the momentum generated by Lt. Evans's visit in October such that when he returned to Cardiff at the end of November 1909 he was in a position to announce that so far Cardiff and the surrounding area had contributed a total of £1,130 towards the Expedition. Moreover, Scott's reservations as to the likely response from Cardiff were now completely allayed. Evans was able to convey to waiting reporters at Cardiff General Station the news that Capt. Scott was so delighted with the support which the Expedition had received from Cardiff that he had decided 'instead of sending the coal by train to London, he will send the *Terra Nova* to coal at Cardiff'[25].

Indeed, there is more than a suggestion that by the time of this visit of Lt. Evans to Cardiff that Scott's hopes of securing sufficient funds for mounting his Expedition were now centred on Cardiff's generosity[26].

That public interest in the challenge for the South Pole was much in evidence received further emphasis with the visit to South Wales by Sir Ernest Shackleton when he lectured at Newport on 29 November and on the following evening addressed the Cardiff Naturalists' Society. There, in the Park Hotel, Shackleton, who enjoyed a reputation as an outstanding public speaker, enthralled a capacity audience with his account of his recent success in coming within 100 miles of the South Pole. Lt. Evans, who was present at the lecture, offered a warm vote of thanks while Shackleton courteously wished the British Antarctic Expedition well. Far from taking the spotlight away from the Scott Expedition, Shackleton's visit served only to reinforce local interest in the forthcoming Expedition[27].

On this visit Lt. Evans spent a busy fortnight with Radcliffe and the Cardiff Docksmen seeking further support for the Antarctic Expedition. By the end of his stay in the city Evans had secured assurances of valuable support in respect of resources, equipment and services for the *Terra Nova*. The *Western Mail* reported that Lt. Evans continued to meet with much success among his 'fellow Cardiffians' such that the Channel Dry Dock had agreed to dry dock and paint the *Terra Nova* free of charge. Mr. Edward Handcock had offered to carry out the necessary towing of the Expedition ship in and out of Cardiff Docks free of charge, while the Docksmen had offered to contribute all the bunker coal required—again free of charge[28]. In accepting these generous offers of assistance from the Cardiff Docksmen, the city was effectively, if not publicly or officially at this stage, designated as the port of departure of the British Antarctic Expedition (1910). In an interview at Cardiff General Station while awaiting the train to return to London at the beginning of December, Evans was able to announce that by now the sum of subscriptions from the area had reached over £1,300, and he took the opportunity to release a telegram he had just received from Capt. Scott, 'Kind support received from Cardiff and neighbourhood much appreciated, and will assist me to push forward work of preparation with greater confidence'[29].

Thus within six weeks of the announcement of the launching of the British Antarctic Expedition (1910), the business community of the City of Cardiff had been forthcoming in cash and resources to such an extent that the benefits to the enterprise of forging a strong Cardiff connexion, so positively and confidently advocated by the editor of the *Western Mail* and so enthusiastically canvassed by Lt.

'Teddy' Evans, were now plain for all to see—especially to Scott himself.

The positive interest in the British Antarctic Expedition within Cardiff—or more precisely by a small group of Cardiff Docksmen—was in marked contrast with the generally low level of support expressed in other towns and cities in England. In these places the response from appeals for funds was disappointing and Scott himself in his fund raising lectures more often than not met with sceptical and sometimes even critical audiences when he endeavoured to persuade them of the scientific importance and value of the Antarctic Expedition.

The general lack of enthusiasm for the project was reflected in the extent of the level of the appeal for contributions. The New Year found the Expedition's coffers far short of the £40,000 minimum sum required to equip the venture. By that date only £11,000 to £12,000 had been received in subscriptions and the chances of substantially improving upon these figures were bleak. Matters were made worse when, in December 1909, the United Kingdom was plunged into a General Election brought about by the final rejection in that month by the House of Lords of the Budget introduced by the Liberal Government in April 1909. Unfortunately for the Antarctic Expedition, the election campaign which ensued turned out to be the longest in modern British political history, taking about ten weeks from the prorogation of Parliament in December until the final polls in February 1910. The General Election thus pushed the Antarctic Expedition out of the headlines and well into the background as far as the general public was concerned such that early in January Scott was obliged to announce that he was suspending the attempt to secure further subscriptions while the election was in progress. It was on this occasion that he announced publicly in London that the *Terra Nova* would depart the United Kingdom from Cardiff[30].

At this low point in the preparations for the Expedition, the Chancellor of the Exchequer, David Lloyd George, announced on behalf of the Liberal Government a grant of £20,000 towards the cost of the Expedition; a sum which was equal to the total cost of Shackleton's recent and successful Expedition[31]. Once again the Cardiff connexion with the British Antarctic Expedition (1910) had a significant and decisive role to play, for there is little doubt that the grant owed much to the persuasive powers of the Editor of the *Western Mail*, W.E. Davies. He was on intimate terms with David Lloyd George and put pressure on his friend, now the Chancellor of the

Exchequer, to persuade a reluctant government to give the Expedition financial support[32]. Furthermore, in his pursuit of government funds through the good offices of Lloyd George, it is highly likely that W.E. Davies was aided and encouraged in his efforts by John Rowland who had close ties with Cardiff and was at this time Private Secretary to the Chancellor of the Exchequer. Rowland had received his early education at Cardiff Technical College, and after having graduated from Aberystwyth served as a teacher at Cardiff Higher Grade School before becoming, in 1906, Private Secretary to Lloyd George when he was appointed President of the Board of Trade[33].

While the government grant came as a welcome addition to the Expedition's funds—especially enabling the completion of the purchase of the *Terra Nova*—the total sum of its finances in January 1910 still fell several thousands of pounds short of the £40,000 required to ensure that the Expedition would be able to depart the United Kingdom on schedule, so that lack of money remained the pressing concern. Indeed, the financial position of the Expedition was so unpromising that early in February 1910 Scott was obliged to announce that if no further money was provided the members of the Expedition would have to be told that they could only be paid for less than half the period of their engagement. In spite of this Scott remained optimistic of the prospects of raising another £8,000 from subscriptions before the Expedition left Britain to say nothing of his hopes for generous donations from the Dominions as the *Terra Nova* travelled out to New Zealand.

With the fund-raising in limbo Scott decided to take himself on a fortnight's visit to Norway from the end of February to try out his motor sledges, upon which so many of his hopes for a successful conquest of the South Pole were based[34]. It was at about this time that Scott, following Shackleton's example, began to hold out the offer of guaranteed inclusion in the Expedition on payment of a substantial sum of money, though in the event only two were appointed in this way, namely, the ill-fated Capt. Oates and the young Oxford graduate, Apsley Cherry-Garrard, later the author of *The Worst Journey in the World*, the classic account of the Antarctic Expedition (1910–13), both of whom donated sums of £1,000 to the Expedition funds[35].

While Scott was in Norway it was confirmed, at the end of February 1910, that the General Election, which had begun in December 1910, had produced an inconclusive result. It was therefore widely expected that a second General Election would have to be called within the next few months, most probably in mid-summer 1910 at just about the time that the *Terra Nova* was scheduled to depart from Cardiff. The protracted political crisis continued to deflect much needed publicity away from the preparation for the British Antarctic Expedition, and especially from the attempts of its organisers and supporters to secure precious additional funds.

Thus the early months of 1910 were a time of frustration, and even despondency, among the supporters of the Expedition. Even in Cardiff it proved almost impossible to attract further financial contributions; a serious situation strikingly demonstrated by the fact that in the six months' period from the occasion of Lt. Evans's exuberant announcement on 1 December 1909 that Cardiff had already contributed just over £1,300, until two days before the departure of the Expedition in June 1910, additional subscriptions came to under £200.

The disappointing return from subscriptions in Cardiff in 1910 was most likely to have been a consequence of a protracted industrial dispute between the Cardiff Docksmen and the Cardiff Coal Trimmers' Union over the contentious issue of payment for Saturday working. It preoccupied the Docks community between March and the departure of the *Terra Nova* in June. While Daniel Radcliffe, as leader of the Cardiff Docksmen, and Alderman John Chappell, as Lord Mayor of Cardiff, shared a common interest in ensuring the success of the City's identification with and promotion of the Antarctic Expedition, they coincidentally found themselves opposing parties in the Docks dispute, since the Lord Mayor's normal occupation was President of the Cardiff Coal Trimmers' Union. In the course of the dispute they served as the most prominent members of the Coal Trimming Disputes Board charged with settling the affair[35a].

In the circumstances, while the *Western Mail* endeavoured to sustain the interest of its readers with details of preparations for the great Antarctic journey, Daniel Radcliffe and his friends concentrated their energies towards securing support from among the Docks community in the way of facilities, resources and equipment, rather than upon canvassing for donations, the sum effects of which, in the event, were to make an incomparable contribution to the Expedition.

If all the difficulties confronting the preparations of the Expedition were not enough, rumours were circulating of rival expeditions being planned to secure the South Pole, and early in 1910 none was more plausible than reports that Commander Peary, who had achieved the North Pole in March 1909, was planning to lead a U.S. attempt on the Antarctic Pole. Fortunately for Scott, Peary decided against attempting the South Pole, and in early summer 1910 he came to Britain on a lecture tour, among the venues for which was Cardiff on 31 May. During the earlier part of the day Commander Peary was received as an honoured guest by the Cardiff Chamber of Commerce in the Exchange Building, while in the evening he delivered a lecture to the Cardiff Naturalists' Society,—'How I found the North Pole'—for which, the *Western Mail* reported, he was to receive payment at what amounted to £3.10s.0d. a minute, a sum which raises the obvious question, what would Scott have commanded had he succeeded in gaining the South Pole for Britain?[36]

Only now in the Spring of 1910 did the civic authorities begin to assume a prominent role in the preparations for the visit of the *Terra Nova* to the city. In April, Lt. Evans, prompted by a visit to him by his friend the Editor of the *Western Mail*, at the British Antarctic Expedition headquarters in London, wrote to the Lord Mayor, Alderman John Chappell outlining the proposed itinerary of the *Terra Nova* which was scheduled to arrive in Cardiff on 10 June. Evans sent Chappell the names of the officers and scientists, but in a post-script, pointed out that, as the party even now had not yet been finalised, 'The names of the officers should not be communicated to the Press in case of changes taking place, but this is the current list as far as Capt. Scott has decided privately'[37]. Alderman Chappell responded by inviting Scott and Evans and their wives to stay as his guests at the Mansion House in the days before the departure of the *Terra Nova*, for which he received a letter of acceptance and thanks on their several behalfs from Lt. Evans[38], though Scott himself wrote a hand-written personal reply to thank the Mayor and the City of Cardiff for all their help[39]:

> British Antarctic Expedition, 1910
> 36 & 38 Victoria Street,
> London S.W.
> 5.5.10

Dear Lord Mayor,

Lieut. Evans has informed me of your kind invitation to Mrs. Scott and myself to stay at the Mansion House during the Terra Nova's visit to Cardiff.

I write to express the great pleasure we shall have in accepting your hospitality. I do not know the exact dates which will find us in your City but I hope to let you know our programme as soon as we can settle the details.

I shall look forward to the opportunity of thanking your citizens for the enthusiastic support which they have given to our enterprise,

believe me,

> Yours very truly,
>
> R. Scott

As if to compound the Expedition's misfortune for failing to achieve maximum publicity during the early weeks of 1910 because of the general election, it received a further blow with the unexpected death of King Edward VII on 6 May, an event which was to dominate the news until his funeral three weeks later. On the other hand the King's death effectively postponed the second general election of 1910 from midsummer, the time of the *Terra Nova's* scheduled time of departure, to later in the year.

The *Terra Nova* departed the India Docks, London, as planned, on 1 June 1910 bound for Cardiff. Scott informed reporters that after the Antarctic party had left Cardiff for New Zealand and Antarctica he would remain in England for about six weeks before setting out to join the *Terra Nova* in order to try to ensure that the financial affairs of the Expedition were in order. He was also hoping to complete a deal with the Central News to give the newspapers the story of the Expedition[40]. Scott reminded the reporters that it had been estimated that £50,000 would be required to cover the minimum costs of the Expedition. It had been planned to attract £40,000, or four-fifths of the sum, in this country and to secure the remaining £10,000 from the various Dominions. At the time of the departure from London the only support which the Expedition had received from the Dominions was a donation of £1,000 from the New Zealand government, and Scott hoped that South Africa and Australia in particular would make up the remainder as the *Terra Nova* called at those countries on its journey to the southern hemisphere. So finance continued to be the outstanding preoccupation faced by Scott. Lt. Evans described his predicament on the eve of her departure from London, 'While we go on a yachting cruise, visiting various parts of the Empire, Captain Scott has the unpleasant duty of going round

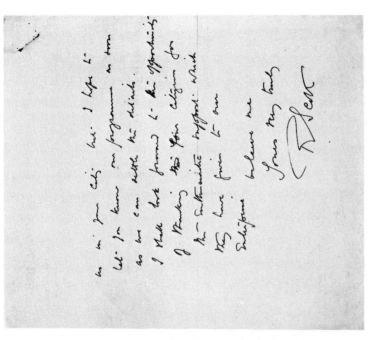

Autograph Letter from Captain Scott to the Lord Mayor of Cardiff.
By kind Permission of the Cardiff City Council.

Photograph taken at the Mansion House, 14 June 1910, and published in the *South Wales Daily News*. From left to right: Captain Scott, the Lord Mayor, Lt. Evans; Mrs Scott, the Lady Mayoress, Mrs Evans. *By permission of the South Glamorgan County Library, Cardiff.*

with the hat in his hand, beseeching people for money to pay his staff'[41].

The journey of the *Terra Nova* from the India Dock, London, to Cardiff was scheduled to take nine days, punctuated by stops along the English Channel. Sir Clements Markham, the veteran Antarctic explorer, accompanied the *Terra Nova* on the first part of the journey to Portsmouth, where she put in to have her compasses checked and set in preparation for the great voyage to the Antarctic.

After visiting Portsmouth and before leaving Spithead the officers and crew of the *Terra Nova* took advantage of a farewell lunch given to them by the Captain and officers of H.M.S. *Invincible*, who presented the expedition with two sledges[42]. On departing from Spithead the *Terra Nova* kept close to Cowes on the Isle of Wight to receive the good wishes of an enthusiastic crowd before sailing on, first to Portland Harbour and then to Weymouth, where, on 8 June at about 5 p.m. Capt. Scott joined the ship for the last leg of her journey to Cardiff[43].

Scott himself had been too preoccupied with Expedition business in London to accompany the ship all the way to Cardiff but the two days he spent aboard the *Terra Nova* afforded him the opportunity to check on the handling of the ship and especially to get to know the officers and crew. Lt. Evans, in command of the *Terra Nova*, was keen to steer her clear of a dense fog which surrounded the waters of the south coast and decided to make for Cardiff as soon as possible[44]. That evening while Lt. Evans pushed the *Terra Nova* ahead, as P.O. Frank Browning recorded in his diary, 'Captain Scott had all hands aft and said that it was his wish that every man should make a will, and also gave us advice regards alloting money'[45]. As it happened, Scott's advice was timely, for in the foggy conditions the *Terra Nova* came near to being involved in a serious, if not calamitous collision, as Browning indicated, 'We eased down, soundings were taken, we were nearly run down by a steamer and had to go full astern to avoid her'[46].

While the *Terra Nova* was making her way to Cardiff, the Lord Mayor, Alderman John Chappell, convened a meeting on 7 June of prominent Docksmen and civic leaders to make plans for assembling a party to go out to meet the *Terra Nova* in the Cardiff Roads and thence to accompany the ship into the Docks on the morning of Friday, 10 June[47]. Chappell's 'committee' also made arrangements for co-ordinating hospitality for the members of the Expedition while the *Terra Nova* was docked in Cardiff.

By a judicious use of sail and steam Lt. Evans brought his ship into Cardiff Roads at 5 p.m. on Thursday, 9 June, some fifteen hours earlier than had been anticipated, whereupon he fixed her position by taking bearings on Flatholm, Monkstone Light and Lavernock Point[48]. Because the arrival of the *Terra Nova* had taken place a day earlier than had been scheduled, the Lord Mayor was obliged hastily to assemble a welcoming party led by himself, accompanied by the President of the Cardiff Chamber of Commerce, Trevor S. Jones, and Daniel Radcliffe, who hurried out to the *Terra Nova* aboard the tug-boat *Mercedes* which came alongside the Expedition ship with her distinctive black wooden hull, ornamented with a white line and with a plain yellow funnel aft, at 8.08 p.m. After a very short meeting with Scott, Evans and members of the crew, the welcoming party departed the ship to prepare to return the following morning as originally planned[49].

Scott's impending visit to the city aboard the *Terra Nova* would be the first occasion on which he had come to Cardiff in connexion with the British Antarctic Expedition (1910), though he had paid one brief visit to the then County Borough of Cardiff some six years earlier in 1904, as a celebrity following his exploits on the National Antarctic Expedition of 1901–4, when he came to deliver a lecture 'Furthest South' in the Park Hotel, on 6 December, having earlier in the evening dined as a distinguished guest of the Council of the County Borough[50].

The miserable weather of June 1910 continued unabated on the morning of Friday, 10 June, to such an extent that Hilda Evans, wife of Lt. 'Teddy' Evans, a guest of the Lord and Lady Mayoress at the Mansion House, decided against going out into the Channel to meet her husband before the ship docked. On this occasion the welcoming party went out to join Scott, Evans and other members of the Expedition aboard *Terra Nova* in Mr. Edmund Handcock's tug *Falcon* and accompany them into Cardiff Docks aboard the *Terra Nova*[51]. Scott was quick to point out to the welcoming party that it was a great pleasure at last to be able to meet with those whose names had become so very familiar to him in recent months and to be able personally to express his thanks for all that the City had contributed to the preparations for the Antarctic journey, for, as he emphasised, 'Cardiff had led the way in helping us with our work of preparation'[52]. At 8.45 a.m., with the welcoming party aboard, the *Terra Nova* weighed anchor in the Cardiff Roads and proceeded towards the Docks with Pilot Jenkins in charge. Finally, at 11.15 a.m., under tow from the tugs *Falcon* and *Plumgarth*, the *Terra Nova* moved into the Roath Dock to be made fast at noon[53] at the berth of the Crown Patent Fuel Company, whose offices were bedecked with bunting and streamers in celebration of the occasion[54].

Throughout the stay of the Expedition party in Cardiff it was the beneficiary of outstanding generosity from the Cardiff Docks community in the provision of equipment, facilities and technical expertise required for the *Terra Nova* and for the Antarctic journey. On the arrival of the *Terra Nova*, for example, Mr. William Jones, Manager of the Channel Dry Dock Company, put his office, including telephone and all facilities, at the disposal of the Expedition[55].

Early in the afternoon of Friday, 10 June, soon after the *Terra Nova* had made fast in the Roath Dock, the task of coaling the ship began[56]. The Expedition was the beneficiary of a valuable gift from the Crown Patent Fuel Company of 300 tons of Crown Patent Fuel, the patent name for compressed briquettes of coal and bitumen. The great advantages of the coal produced by this process were that it occupied one-third less space than ordinary coal, and in extremely hot or cold temperatures it retained its density compared with ordinary coal which depreciated by between 30 and 40 per cent. Scott had had previous experience of the merits of this product as 200 tons of Crown Patent Fuel had been supplied to the Admiralty for the *Discovery* Expedition of 1901–4[57].

Scott was keen to ensure that this part of the coaling of the ship should be completed by Friday afternoon and he personally supervised the operation, after which all hands were landed while the ship was fumigated to clear away any accumulated coal dust[58].

With the successful completion of this stage of the coaling operation, the ship was cleaned and tidied and the ship's company were given the evening off and most of them, led by Lt. Evans, took the opportunity of the offer of the acting Manager of the Empire Theatre to attend the second performance of the Music Hall in the company of the Lord Mayor and Lady Mayoress[59].

Scott returned to London on Friday evening and preparations during the remainder of the weekend were supervised by Lt. Evans. On Saturday morning the *Terra Nova* was moved to the East Bute Dock to take on board 100 tons of steam coal, 50 tons of which were the gift of the Ynyshir Colliery Company and 50 tons the gift of Messrs Insole and Sons, making just over 400 tons of coal in all[60].

With the completion of coaling of the *Terra Nova* on Saturday morning, most of the officers and crew were given leave of absence

The *Terra Nova* taking on Crown Patent Fuel on Roath Dock, 10 June 1910.
By kind permission of the National Museum of Wales

for the remainder of the weekend before reporting back in time to make final preparations on Monday morning. Some of the Expeditionary party took the chance to say their farewells to their families, while some of the officers took advantage of the hospitality offered by leading Docksmen by joining them in their homes for the weekend. Kathleen Scott, Lt. Evans and his wife stayed as guests of the Lord Mayor and Lady Mayoress in the Mansion House, while his namesake, the ill-fated P.O. Edgar Evans, the Expedition's equipment officer who had joined the *Terra Nova* from his home in Rhosili, near Swansea, took the opportunity to say goodbye to his wife Lois and family and some of his relations in the Cardiff area[61]. Those members of the Expedition who had a free evening on Saturday joined a party including Mrs. Scott which, at the invitation of the Manager, W.A. Jackson, attended a variety show at the Palace Theatre Hippodrome during the course of which Lt. Evans delivered a short speech to thank the people of Cardiff for their support[62].

The *Terra Nova* attracted vast crowds of sightseers to Cardiff Docks on the Sunday but it seems that only 100 or so visitors felt able to pay the 2s.6d. required for admission to inspect the ship, the total revenues from which, £13.8s.11d., were donated to the Cardiff Royal Infirmary[63].

Scott returned from London on Sunday to join his wife, Lt. Evans and Mrs. Evans as guests of the Lord Mayor and the Lady Mayoress at the Mansion House. This enabled Scott to be on hand to oversee with Evans the final details of the preparation of the *Terra Nova*. Monday and Tuesday, 13 and 14 June 1910, were days of hectic activity about the *Terra Nova* during the day and of notable social gatherings in the evenings. P.O. Frank Browning wrote at the time that all hands were kept busy storing gear and preparing the ship for sea[64].

During these days there was stored most of the Expedition's equipment, including scientific equipment, and necessities for the smooth running of the ship, a good proportion of which was supplied by the Cardiff businessmen or local well-wishers, or as a result of Cardiff-based initiatives. The largest bulk item secured at this stage was all the oil required for the *Terra Nova*, some 500 gallons of engine oil and colza or lamp oil, supplied as a gift from the American-based Vacuum Oil Company. It was a gift which derived from the entreaties of John Lewis, son of Gethin Lewis and brother of Percy, Lt. Evans's friend, who persuaded Mr. R.G. Prizer, the

Cardiff representative of the Vacuum Oil Company, to prevail upon his London superiors to authorise the free supply of oil for the ship[65].

The Welsh Tin Plate Company, for example, presented the Expedition with virtually all of its cooking utensils and mess equipment reckoned to be worth £100[66]. The League of Empire, Newport Branch, donated 10 guineas for the purchase of three aneroid barometers[67]. Lt. Evans was able to announce that a local well-wisher had presented the crew of the *Terra Nova* with 100 dozen of Stone's ginger wine for their journey[68]. A number of items of technical equipment valuable for the *Terra Nova* arrived from their suppliers as gifts to the Expedition, some of which were as a result of last minute requests from the ship's Chief Engineer, Lt. Edgar Riley, from Cardiff[69].

The tents and sleeping bags, the dogs and ponies had been financed mainly by contributions from various schools in England and Wales, among which items the sleeping bag of Lt. Evans was supplied by Cowbridge School, and that of Capt. Scott by the County School, Cardigan[70].

By Tuesday afternoon most of the equipment and stores necessary for the Polar Expedition had been taken on board the *Terra Nova* and stowed away. It was not until the vessel reached New Zealand, however, when the dogs, ponies, motor tractors and seven members of the Expedition party joined the ship at Lyttleton, that the British Antarctic Expedition was brought up to its full complement of men, animals and equipment[71].

To all outward appearances the final preparations of the *Terra Nova*, hectic though they were, had proceeded according to plan. However, unknown to few outside the ship's company serious leaks developed in the *Terra Nova* during the final two days in which she lay in Cardiff. The leaks occurred following the coaling of the *Terra Nova* at the week-end such that with this additional weight—together with all the equipment taken on board while the ship was in Cardiff—it was observed that the vessel settled lower in the water than anticipated, thus exposing the weakness of timbers usually above the waterline. It was thought at the time that the main source of the leaks was in the timbers in the bows of the ship and much effort was spent in caulking and cementing them to try to ensure a prompt departure from Cardiff. The condition of the *Terra Nova* must have been a matter of great concern to the leaders of the Expedition, for it cast doubts on the sea-worthiness of the vessel and might even have posed a serious threat to the viability of the attempt on the Antarctic Pole. Be that as it may, it is clear that the vessel was about to depart from Cardiff carrying more weight in coal, equipment and personnel than was desirable. Thus the strategem of registering the *Terra Nova* as a yacht and thereby avoiding Board of Trade regulations, served its purpose, albeit at considerable danger to the safety of the ship.

Lt. Evans responded to persistent questioning by a *Western Mail* reporter as to the substance of rumours about the condition of the *Terra Nova* by characterising them as 'trifles'[72]. In fact, the leaks were far more serious than Evans was prepared to concede, anxious, doubtless, to ensure that the ship departed the United Kingdom on time and apparently not disposed to countenance any changes in the Expedition's plans.

On the morning of the departure of the Expedition the *South Wales Daily News* carried a report which suggested that the leaks—which, it said, had developed during the passage of the ship from London to Cardiff—had resulted from the use of rivets too small for the holes in the metal plates which had been placed in position in the bows of the ship in order to strengthen the vessel for its journeys in the ice-ridden Antarctic waters[73]. Whatever the veracity of this report there remained widespread uncertainty as to the true nature and extent of the leaks in the *Terra Nova*. There was no doubt, however, that since the completion of the coaling of the *Terra Nova* on Saturday morning the pressure of the water had built up such that the crew had been engaged in pumping operations two or three times a day. One of the crew told the reporter that although the ship would leave Cardiff as scheduled all the plates would probably be removed and refitted when the *Terra Nova* reached New Zealand, and added that 'the pumping operations will give us extensive work on the passage—perhaps three or four hours out of every 12'. P.O. Keohane recorded in his private log, or diary, at the time, that the leaks were very bad until extensive last minute caulking of the ship's bows was carried out[74], probably by the Mercantile Pontoon Co., under the direction of its manager, Mr. Philip L. Lusden[75].

Although in the event it became apparent that the sources of the leaks had been neither located nor corrected satisfactorily while the *Terra Nova* lay in Cardiff, the caulking of the timbers and other hurried repairs were sufficient to enable the vessel to depart on time. Lt. Evans in his book, *South with Scott*, was full of praise for the contribution made by Cardiff Docksmen to the preparation of the *Terra*

Nova during these days prior to the departure of the Expedition. 'We were welcomed by the citizens of the great Welsh port with enthusiasm. Free docking, free coal, defects made good for nothing, an office and staff placed at our disposal, in fact everything was done with an open handed generosity'[76].

The rumours of leaks in the *Terra Nova* rather deflected attention from the final efforts of Lt. Evans before he departed from Cardiff to counter the views of those who saw no purpose in polar exploration because it had no commercial advantages. In his last interview with a local journalist Evans endeavoured to persuade him and his readers that the British had been slow, compared with the Norwegians, to appreciate and exploit the natural resources of the Antarctic regions and argued that the current Expedition provided an outstanding opportunity to redress the situation[77].

That evening, Monday, 13 June, the officers of the British Antarctic Expedition (1910) led by Capt. Scott were entertained as guests of the Cardiff Chamber of Commerce at a grand farewell dinner given in their honour at the Royal Hotel, St. Mary Street, while the crew were given dinner by the Chamber of Commerce at the nearby Barry's Hotel further down St. Mary Street, after which they joined the officers and leading members of the Cardiff business community at the Royal Hotel.

Preparations for the evening of 13 June were begun as recently as the preceding week commencing with the establishment on 8 June of a sub-committee of the Chamber of Commerce 'to make arrangements for the entertainment of the officers and crew of the Terra Nova', seemingly as a response by the commercial community to an earlier initiative by the City authorities to hold a civic reception on Tuesday, 14 June. The six man sub-committee comprised the Chairman of the Chamber of Commerce, Trevor S. Jones, and included Daniel Radcliffe and two other prominent shipowners, T.E. Morel, the current Chairman of the Cardiff Shipowners' Association and Edward Nicoll. The Secretary of the Chamber of Commerce, W.R. Hawkins, was detailed to make preparations for the menus, and the Committee soon decided that the 7s.6d. menu, including wine, submitted by the Royal Hotel and the 2s.6d. menu submitted by Barry's Hotel should be accepted for the respective dinners. Morel and Nicoll, who in the event were joined by W.R. Hawkins, volunteered to represent the Chamber of Commerce at dinner with 28 members of the crew at Barry's Hotel. R.A. Morgan was asked to make arrangements for the smoking concert at the Royal Hotel which, it was hoped, might consist of 'two comic singers and a harpist'.

Trevor S. Jones was prepared to donate £25 towards the cost of the entertainments and the Committee resolved that invitations to attend the dinner at the Royal Hotel should be sent to every member of the Chamber of Commerce indicating that the cost of the evening's festivities would not exceed three guineas per ticket. Finally, the Committee agreed to ask Edward North to arrange for the provision of a flag emblazoned with the arms of the City of Cardiff for presentation as a gift to the Antarctic Expedition at the dinner[78].

Nearly 100 guests assembled at 6.30 p.m. to enjoy a splendid dinner in the Alexandra Room[79] at the Royal Hotel in which the purpose of the occasion was celebrated in some of the principal items on the menu, notably fillets of beef *Terra Nova*; soufflé Capt. Scott and South Pole ice pudding, all of which was eaten to the discreet accompaniment of F.G. Roberts's String Band who opened its repertoire with a rendering of 'The Hero of the South'[80].

The toast to the health of Capt. Scott was proposed by the Chairman of the Cardiff Chamber of Commerce, Trevor S. Jones. In his reply, Capt. Scott was understandably generous in his thanks for the help and support which had been afforded the Expedition by the people of Cardiff. He paid tribute to Welsh enterprise and said that he would rather sail from Cardiff than from any port in the world, where he found the best coal, the best facilities and the best backing any explorer could hope for. Indeed, as Scott was glad to acknowledge 'they could not have faced the strain of preparation except for the support they had received from South Wales'.

The main burden of speaking on behalf of the Expedition fell upon Lt. Evans, who paid tribute to the help he had received from Cardiff and especially from Daniel Radcliffe, his brother-in-law, W.J. Tatem, Mr. Gethin Lewis, the Lord Mayor (John Chappell) and his immediate predecessor, (Alderman Lewis Morgan), for arranging the provision of resources, for helping to secure funds, and for making arrangements for the hospitality of the Expedition party while its members were in Cardiff. Evans pointed out that, as of that evening, because of the precarious state of the finances of the Expedition, Capt. Scott was personally liable for the wages bill such that many members of the Expedition would embark for the Antarctic without the complete assurance of being paid their wages. Indeed, Scott had been forced to arrange for him to take command of the *Terra Nova* on its journey to the Expedition's base in New

Zealand, while he remained in London to face responsibility for collecting sufficient money for the Expedition.

On a lighter note, Evans amused his audience by claiming that he had acquired his business instincts in Cardiff and ended by making one final appeal to those present who could afford it, to 'stump up' with funds.

There followed a break in the proceedings for about a half-an-hour for a musical interlude during which Daniel Radcliffe went in person to Barry's Restaurant to invite the members of the crew, who included P.O. Edgar Evans, to join with the officers and members of the Chamber of Commerce at a smoking concert at the Royal Hotel.

There was on display at the dinner a magnificent Welsh flag made by James Howell and offered the Expedition via Lt. Evans during his first fund raising visit to Cardiff in November 1909. After everyone was assembled once again, Trevor S. Jones, Chairman of the dinner, called upon the Lord Mayor to present Scott with a second flag bearing the arms of the City of Cardiff, probably a gift of Edward Nicoll[81] which was entrusted to the care of P.O. Edgar 'Taffy' Evans. Edgar Evans, an old friend and comrade of Scott's, during the proceedings took up an honoured position at the 'smoker' when, at Scott's behest, he sat between the Expedition's leader and the Lord Mayor.

The speeches and conversations at the dinner abounded with jokey and mock-serious allusions to the South Pole. The Lord Mayor, for example, in entrusting the Cardiff flag to the care of P.O. Evans, hoped that it would eventually be nailed to the Pole. In amongst all the banter, however, there were suggestions that a number of businessmen present were not entirely sure what the Expedition was intended to achieve or exactly where or what the South Pole actually was. David M'Fall the special *Western Mail* correspondent present at the Royal Hotel reported one such conversation with a dinner table companion—'One enthusiastic gentleman on my left—all he knows about the vessel is how much profit he can get by coaling one— . . . made a whispered bargain with one of the *Terra Nova's* crew to chip off and smuggle through a piece of the Pole for his private collection'.

In his words of thanks to the Lord Mayor for the gift of the flag of the City of Cardiff, Capt. Scott promised the assembled guests that the *Terra Nova* would depart the Docks with the flag flying and that it would be hoisted again at the South Pole. 'I assure you we shall not forget our welcome in Cardiff nor this flag. The warmth of our welcome in Cardiff will inspire us in what I really believe is a great work'.

At Scott's invitation Seaman Evans was invited to say a few words. He took the opportunity to praise the leadership of Capt. Scott and made it clear that no one else could have persuaded him to return to the Antarctic. For Scott's benefit Evans translated the two Welsh mottos on the Cardiff flag as: 'Awake the day' and 'The Welsh Dragon leads the van'. Entering into the spirit of the occasion, Evans asked that if the Expedition returned with the pole it might be installed in Swansea rather than in the National Museum in Cardiff. Evans ended by expressing the hope that 'if we ever do come back we hope to meet you in Cardiff'.

The evening was drawing to a close but at this point in the proceedings Daniel Radcliffe, 'amid a scene of great enthusiasm' announced that he would donate £500 to the Expedition: W.J. Tatem followed with a donation of £52.10s.0d. Their example was followed by others so that within fifteen minutes the Expedition acquired nearly £1,000—actually £981—to add to its funds.

The gifts of money generated by Radcliffe's initiative, Lt. Evans was able to announce, were more than sufficient to put Cardiff ahead of Manchester, its nearest rival, as the leading provider of funds from the whole of the United Kingdom. It was plain to all that these contributions went a long way towards relieving Scott of the anxiety— to say nothing of the embarrassment—of having to preside over the departure of the British Antarctic Expedition from the United Kingdom unable to guarantee the wages of most of his officers and crew.

Scott made no public statement at the dinner in response to this remarkable expression of support for the Antarctic Expedition. It seems clear, however, that in the course of his private thanks to the principal benefactors at the dinner, he conveyed his personal view that in recognition of the outstanding contribution of Cardiff towards ensuring the viability of the Expedition, the City of Cardiff should be designated the United Kingdom port to which the *Terra Nova* should return from her Antarctic journey. The following day he made public his thoughts on the matter.

All present at the Royal Hotel had every reason to entertain optimistic hopes for the success of the British Antarctic Expedition (1910). The Cardiff Docksmen, in particular, were entitled to take satisfaction at the public acknowledgement by Capt. Scott of the extent to which their contributions in money and resources had served to ensure that the Expedition should become a viable project, and to reflect on the prestige and esteem which had accrued to them and their City as a result of the Cardiff connexion.

The penultimate day of the *Terra Nova's* stay in Cardiff was a round of frantic last minute preparations and further social engagements. Scott and Evans attended a farewell lunch at the Cardiff Exchange where, surrounded by Daniel Radcliffe and his close colleagues, Scott made a point of elaborating on his remarks of the previous evening to reassure them that it was Cardiff's right to receive the *Terra Nova* on her return. In a brief address of thanks to the members of the Exchange, Lt. Evans revealed that at the beginning of his fund raising activities in Cardiff he had advised Capt. Scott that he hoped to raise £1,000 in Wales[82]. In the event, with the addition of the contributions offered at the Royal Hotel the previous evening, the funds of the British Antarctic Expedition had received more than twice that sum from the City. Furthermore, it seems that the total sum of contributions attracted in Cardiff came to £2,500, a figure of £500 more than Manchester[83].

In the Docks the *Terra Nova* was a hive of activity. The ship was inundated with sightseers and well wishers while the ship's company made every effort to clean it down in preparation for its departure the following day. Only those most closely associated with the promotion of the Antarctic Expedition in Cardiff were allowed aboard. One such was Daniel Radcliffe who accompanied Scott back from the Exchange and went aboard the *Terra Nova* personally to wish every member of the crew good luck and to present each one with a signed photograph of himself[84].

On the evening of Tuesday, 14 June—to which reference was made in the *Western Mail* as the eve of the departure of the Expedition from 'England's shores'—it was the turn of the civic authorities to offer the Expeditionary party a grand farewell reception in the City Hall at the invitation of the Lord Mayor, Alderman John Chappell.

The civic reception was a considerable occasion for which about 800 invitations had been issued. It was very much a Cardiff affair though invitations had been sent to members of the British Antarctic Committee such as Lord Strathcona, Sir Edgar Speyer, and the President of the Royal Geographical Society, Major Leonard Darwin, all of whom declined to attend. Sir Clements Markham, Scott's mentor, perhaps by oversight rather than design, was not issued with an invitation[85].

All the assembled guests at the buffet reception were afforded their last opportunity to offer their good wishes to the members of the British Antarctic Expedition for their success in being the first to the unconquered South Pole. The background music for the buffet was provided by Madame Hughes-Thomas's Royal Welsh Ladies' Choir. It was not an occasion for formal speech making, though Scott confined himself to a few well chosen words of thanks for the support which the Expedition had received from the Cardiff area. He made the best of the opportunity of the well attended gathering to announce that it was the unanimous desire of the officers and crew that if the Expedition should make history by reaching its goal, the *Terra Nova* should return to Cardiff in preference to any other port in the United Kingdom[86].

There were suggestions that a number of members of the Expedition indulged themselves on their final two nights in Cardiff. P.O. Edgar Evans enjoyed rather too much of the hospitality on offer at the Mayor's reception and become so 'tight' that six men had to carry him back to the *Terra Nova*[87], a performance which was repeated before the Expedition departed from New Zealand in November 1910. Though Edgar Evans was perhaps the worst, and certainly the only identified miscreant, there is a strong suggestion that other members of the Expedition may have misbehaved themselves while in Cardiff. The behaviour of some of the members of the Expeditionary party left a clear impression on Lt. Bowers, who died along with Scott on the return from the Pole. In a letter he wrote to Kathleen Scott from the Expedition's winter quarters in Antarctica in October 1911, some sixteen months after having left Cardiff, he observed that their experiences in the Antarctic up to that time had helped 'us to approach the job—with, in the case of some of us—a little less of that spirit that did not do us credit on our departure from Cardiff'[88]. However, the only member of the Expeditionary party to be discharged, probably on the morning of departure, was Leading Stoker, Able Seaman W.H. Schermuley, for what was described as leave breaking[89].

The *Terra Nova* was scheduled to leave Cardiff between 12 noon and 1 p.m. on Wednesday, 15 June 1910. The *Western Mail* of that morning, besides carrying a report of the civic reception of the previous evening, printed a number of messages wishing the Expedition every success from figures as diverse as Sir Clements Markham, Lord Strathcona, the Chancellor of the Exchequer, Lloyd George, together with local worthies such as the Principal of the local University College.

Before the vessel departed Roath Dock basin a number of Cardiff dignitaries, as well as local subscribers to the funds of the Expedition, led by the Lord Mayor and Daniel Radcliffe, went aboard to accompany the *Terra Nova* into the Channel and to pay their personal farewells to the Expeditionary party[90]. Capt. Oates was unfairly dismissive of the Lord Mayor and his guests: 'The Mayor and his crowd came on board and I never saw such a mob—they are Labour Socialists'[90a]. Privileged to be aboard the *Terra Nova* was Sarah, the twenty-two years old niece of P.O. Edgar Evans who had travelled from Swansea to say goodbye to her uncle. Seaman Evans was held in high regard by Scott, and, as his niece recalled, Capt. Scott called her uncle to his cabin to receive the good wishes of the Lord Mayor of Cardiff as the *Terra Nova* departed the city[91].

At about 1 o'clock with the tug *Falcon* attached to the bow and the tug the *Bantam Cock* fastened to the stern, the *Terra Nova* was taken in tow and passed through the lock gates to the cheers of vast crowds of well wishers[92]. One member of the crew of the *Terra Nova* had the misfortune to be knocked overboard in the excitement but he managed to swim alongside before being restored to the safety of the ship.

Dr. Edward Wilson, Chief Scientist and confidant of Scott, who, together with his leader, lost his life at the Pole, described the send-off as 'very enthusiastic, enormous crowds having collected at every available post to cheer and fire guns and detonators, and to make a perfectly hideous din with sirens and hooters, of which Cardiff seems to possess an infinite number'[93].

Once clear of the Docks the *Terra Nova* moved out into the Channel escorted by a fleet of small craft crowded with sightseers and well-wishers. Flanked by pleasure steamers, with the *Devonia*—the upper deck of which had been placed by the directors of the Red Funnel Line at the disposal of members of the Council of the Chamber of Commerce and of the City Council[94]—on the starboard side and the *Ravenswood* on the port side, the Expedition ship proceeded slowly until she came into line with Penarth Pier where the tugs were dispensed with and she began to sail under her own steam. Lt. Evans entered into the spirit of the occasion when, in response to repeated calls from the passengers aboard the *Devonia* and the *Ravenswood*, he spoke to them through a megaphone saying, 'My heart is too full of words to say thank you'.

With the striking similarity in the words to describe both the recent problems confronting the *Terra Nova* in Cardiff Docks and the Welsh emblem, the departure of the ship was redolent with opportunity for idle banter and school-boy puns, as was reflected in Lt. Evans's published recollection of the send-off from Cardiff, 'We hoisted the Cardiff flag at the fore and the Welsh flag at the mizen—some wag pointed to the flag and asked why we had not a leek under it, and I felt bound to reply that we had a leak in the forepeak'[95].

It was perhaps in response to this exchange that one of the officers of the *Terra Nova* took it upon himself to hoist a couple of large leeks with the Welsh flag which brought vociferous cheers from the passengers on the pleasure boats. Councillor S.W. Courtis, not to be outdone, was reported to have caused a great deal of laughter by exclaiming to Lt. Evans, 'We hope you have left the Welsh "leak" behind'.

The *Devonia* was the first boat to part company with the *Terra Nova* with the Post Office band wishing the Expedition goodbye with a rendering of *Hen Wlad fy Nhadau*. A few minutes later the *Ravenswood* turned back towards Cardiff with the Cardiff Artillery band wishing the Expedition farewell by playing *Auld Lang Syne*. The last craft to leave the *Terra Nova's* side was Mr. W.H. Tuke's tug, *Lady Morgan*, which had been commissioned for the occasion by Mr. W.T. Symonds, J.P., and a party of friends.

The Lord Mayor's party remained aboard the *Terra Nova* as far as Breaksea Lightship before their final parting in late afternoon aboard the tug *Falcon* accompanied by Capt. and Mrs. Scott and Mrs. Evans. Three years later Daniel Radcliffe recalled Scott's prophetic last words as he departed the *Terra Nova*, 'I will reach the South Pole or I will never come back again'[96].

Terra Nova remained in sight until she passed Nash Lighthouse, and Lt. Evans, entering into the spirit of the occasion and possibly even acting upon a suggestion made by a pseudonymous correspondent, 'Porthcawlite', in a letter published in *Western Mail* on the eve of departure[97], kept the ship close to the Welsh coastline so that the people of the Vale of Glamorgan might have a chance to see the ship. After having returned to Pier Head, Capt. and Mrs. Scott and Mrs. Evans paid a brief visit to the Mansion House with the Lord Mayor and Lady Mayoress of Cardiff to take leave of their hosts where, 'after partaking of tea, they left for London'[98].

The day after the departure of the *Terra Nova* the *Western Mail* published the contents of a letter composed by Scott aboard the ship just before the Expeditionary party left Cardiff which he handed per-

sonally to the Lord Mayor, Alderman John Chappell, thanking the
people of Cardiff for their support[99].

My Dear Lord Mayor,
   I hasten to express the warm thanks of myself and the officers and
men of the Terra Nova to the citizens of Cardiff and South Wales for
the magnificent send-off which the expedition has received on its
departure from Cardiff, as well as for the hospitality with which we
have been entertained in your city.
   We feel that such an expression of warm sympathy and hearty
good will is an inspiration for success, and we wish to assure our
many friends in Wales that we shall endeavour to deserve the confidence they repose in us and to merit the welcome which we know is
in store when our work is done and the Terra Nova returns to Cardiff.
   With the addition of my thanks for your personal kindness,
      Believe me, my dear Lord Mayor,
                              Yours very sincerely,
                              R. Scott

   The British Antarctic Expedition had got under way on time but
even now funds remained Scott's most pressing concern. On the day
following the exciting departure of the Expedition from Cardiff,
Scott, a Devonian by birth, was entertained in London as the guest
of the London Devonian Association, where he spoke warmly of
Cardiff's support for his enterprise, 'large sums of money had been
subscribed in Cardiff but they needed more'[100]. In fact, as Scott
himself must have feared, now that the *Terra Nova* had left for the
South there was little likelihood of acquiring any further funds in the
six weeks that remained before he left to join the ship in South
Africa.
   It was only now, 18 June 1910, when Scott was back in London,
that he found time to write a letter of thanks to W.E. Davies, Editor
of the *Western Mail*, not published at the time, which he prefaced by
expressing his regret that because of the pressure of Expedition business while he was in Cardiff he had not had the opportunity to offer
sufficient personal thanks to many people in the city[101].
   I shall be glad to assure your readers that neither particular acts of

kindness nor the warm general encouragement that we have received from South Wales will be forgotten.

But I should be lacking in gratitude especially if I did not, even at this late date, express my appreciation of the particular service which has been rendered to our cause by the *Western Mail*.

Throughout the preparation of the Expedition you have freely used your great influence to interest the public in the venture and to gain its support for our needs.

I must gratefully recognise that this great assistance has been given freely from a patriotic desire to advance a national undertaking.

Believe me,

Yours very truly,

R. Scott, R.N.

The reluctance of the British public to provide adequate funds for the British Antarctic Expedition (1910) stands in marked contrast to the enthusiastic and dedicated support which the enterprise received from the Cardiff business community in its provision of subscriptions, resources and facilities on a scale quite unequalled by any town or group of backers anywhere in Britain. Daniel Radcliffe, in taking upon himself the leadership of the Cardiff Docksmen in support of the Expedition, through his personal donations—amounting to about one fifth of the total subscriptions deriving from the Cardiff area—his commitment and tireless campaigning, probably contributed more towards the Expedition than anyone in the United Kingdom, as Lt. Evans (having become Commander Evans) pointed out when he returned the *Terra Nova* to Cardiff from the Antarctic in June 1913[102]. Though less tangible and less public than that of Daniel Radcliffe, it could be said that the contribution of W.E. Davies, Editor of the *Western Mail*, as the inspiration behind the Cardiff connexion with the Scott Expedition, was in its own way scarcely less significant.

The Cardiff connexion with the British Antarctic Expedition (1910) had produced the largest contribution secured by way of subscriptions amounting to £2,500 out of a total sum of about £14,000[103]. Furthermore, the Cardiff Docksmen had provided the lion's share of the resources, equipment, technical facilities and expertise for the *Terra Nova*, so that in financial terms the overall contribution from Cardiff might well have been in the region of £5,000[104], the sort of financial outlay which the funds of the

Expedition would have been quite unable to bear. In addition, it should be remembered, the government grant of £20,000 was made to the Expedition in large measure as a result of Cardiff-inspired influence by way of the Editor of the *Western Mail* and John Rowland upon the Chancellor of the Exchequer, David Lloyd George.

Having departed from Cardiff in June 1910, and on the assumption of the most favourable weather conditions and general good fortune attending the endeavours of the explorers, it was widely held that it would take Scott and his Expeditionary party at least two years to accomplish the South Pole and return to Cardiff, as Scott had promised. For much of the time the main expeditionary party would be out of contact with the civilised world, but wherever practicable the connexion between the British Antarctic Expedition and Cardiff was maintained largely through the efforts of Lt. Edward Evans who showed himself a faithful correspondent with his Cardiff friends, and especially with Daniel Radcliffe and Percy Lewis. Evans's surviving Cardiff correspondence reflects his attachment to Cardiff and his deep appreciation of the significance of the connexion between the City and the Antarctic Expedition—and particularly for the efforts of Daniel Radcliffe and his friends in the Cardiff Docks community, without whom it is more than likely that the British Antarctic Expedition (1910) would not have been in a fit state of preparation to depart the United Kingdom on time to engage in the historic attempt to secure the South Pole.

II
The Cardiff connexion maintained

Eight days out of Cardiff, on 23 June 1910, the *Terra Nova* reached Funchal, Madeira, her first port of call. From there Lt. Evans sent Daniel Radcliffe a short letter to let him know that so far all was well.[105] 'We made a very good passage with light fair winds averaging a good 7 knots. This is not a liner's speed, but like the bloody old tortoise we get there all the same . . .

The fo'c'sle was nicely cleaned up and on one of the mess tables was your photograph.

Two years and two months old boy and your grateful friend Teddy will be looking out for a hearty handshake with you.

It seems a long time'.

At sea between Madeira and South Africa, at some point 1500 miles from Simonstown, Evans had time to write a more detailed letter to Radcliffe.[106]

'This ship is no "flyer" but she is better than my last Antarctic ship the "Morning" . . . You wouldn't know the "Terra Nova" now, we have put some good work into her and she is as clean and in order as a man-of-war. None of that damn top hamper that was such an eye-sore to me at Cardiff'.

Evans took the opportunity to demonstrate the high regard in which Radcliffe was held by the ship's crew by informing him that a framed copy of the photograph which Radcliffe had presented to each of the crew in Cardiff now occupied a prominent position in the fo'c'sle. 'I should value one myself very much if you could send it to Lyttleton, New Zealand . . .

That leak is not so bad now, but we shall have to dock in New Zealand before going South. Remember me very kindly to Bill Tatem, Joe Fraser, Channel Jones, your brother Henry and all the boys I know. I often think of the cheery company at lunch at the corner table'—at the restaurant in the Exchange Building, Cardiff.

On her journey to New Zealand and the Antarctic because the *Terra Nova* was overloaded and because, wherever possible in order to conserve coal, she proceeded under sail, the ship fell behind schedule. In a letter to his friend Percy Lewis written 'at sea', 13

August 1910, Lt. Evans referred to the slow progress of the *Terra Nova* which had become a matter of some concern between Madeira and Simonstown.[107]

'We are 500 miles from Simonstown and we shall be a fortnight overdue . . . We counted on her steaming 7 knots easily, but she only does 6 and she won't sail well . . . the day we left [Madeira] we got into the N.E. trades, stopped engines, and sailed for 11 days'.

Corroboration as to the slow progress of the ship was supplied by Lt. H. Rennick R.N., watch keeper of the *Terra Nova*, in a letter to Daniel Radcliffe with whom he probably stayed when the *Terra Nova* was docked in Cardiff. He was able to convey sailing plans of the *Terra Nova* which were not part of the original itinerary.[108]

'We are now nearing Capetown after a spell of 16 days overdue. We can't get any speed out of the old bug trap. It is only by hanging on to and risking canvas that we can manage 9 knots out of her under sail'., adding significantly, 'Owing to being delayed in our programme we are cutting out Melbourne and Sydney and going from the Cape to Lyttleton (42 days sea passage)'.

When the *Terra Nova* reached Simonstown on 15 August 1910, two weeks later than planned, the Expeditionary party was met by Scott who was proceeding to New Zealand by mail steamer with his wife and the wives of Lt. Evans and Dr. Wilson.

Scott's stopover in South Africa was no time for rest and relaxation. As usual he was obliged to canvass for precious funds for the Expedition which produced a disappointing donation of £500 from the South African government and a few private subscriptions, the total of which came to less than £900.[109]

Despite the demands on his time Scott remained acutely conscious of any help which had been afforded the Expedition by his friends in Cardiff and while at Simonstown he found time to convey his thanks to the Secretary of the Sailors' Rest, near Canal Wharf, for having provided accommodation and recreation for most of his crew while the *Terra Nova* was docked in Cardiff, as well as offering his thanks for the receipt of a number of photographs illustrating the event.[110] At the same time back in Cardiff memories of the City's connexion with the British Antarctic Expedition were commemorated with the presentation to the City by Alderman Chappell of a framed photograph of the departure of the *Terra Nova* from the City.[111]

It was clear that the decision to 'cut out Melbourne' was taken without Scott's approval, and it is likely that because of this, while at Simonstown, he changed his plans to continue his journey to Australia by passenger liner and decided to take command of the *Terra Nova* when she departed Simons Bay bound for Melbourne on 2 September 1910[112] anxious doubtless not to pass up the opportunity of the presence of the ship to secure donations from Australia.

At the beginning of October, while in the South Indian Ocean, some 1740 miles from Melbourne, Lt. Evans prepared another letter for despatch to Daniel Radcliffe.[113]

'It is Sunday to-day and at supper we are drinking the toast of absent friends, coupled with the name of Dan Radcliffe, so I am writing to you as befits the occasion . . . I will write you a farewell letter if I can before we leave New Zealand, but if by chance you do not hear again for many months remember that there are many fine men here forward and aft who have reason to be grateful to Dan Radcliffe, and who are proud to have him as their friend.

And I, dear Old Dan, am more grateful and more attached to you than any of them, and that says a great deal'.

Scott's presence on board the *Terra Nova* from South Africa to Australia did nothing to speed up the ship such that when she reached Melbourne on 12 October 1910, she was by then one month behind schedule. It was there that Scott found waiting a telegram from the Norwegian explorer Roald Amundsen informing him that he had turned his attention to seeking the South Pole. 'Beg leave to inform you proceeding Antarctic Amundsen'. Scott himself stayed in Melbourne for a few days for what Lt. Evans described as 'yet another begging campaign', in the course of which he managed to wrest £2,500 from a reluctant Australian government; half of what he had hoped for.

While Scott attended to business in Australia the *Terra Nova* proceeded on to Lyttleton Harbour, New Zealand, once again under the command of Lt. Evans, which destination it reached on 28 October. There Scott joined the British Antarctic Expedition having proceeded on to New Zealand by passenger boat.

At Lyttleton attempts were made to locate and repair the leak in the *Terra Nova* which had been first revealed in Cardiff and had continued to cause concern throughout the ship's voyage to New Zealand. The repair work was entrusted to Mr. J.H. Miller of Lyttleton, who reported that the hasty caulking and repairs carried out in Cardiff were a bad job.[114]

In spite of the extensive repairs effected by Miller, leaks still occurred, the problems arising from which were compounded by the inefficiency of the pumps which had been evident from early in the

Terra Nova's voyage.[115] The leaks let in on average up to two feet of
water per watch which required continuous work rotas from all
members of the Expedition party. Lt. Evans himself admitted
several years later that the leaking seams involved half-an-hour to an
hour's pumping with each watch.[116]

While at Lyttleton, and before departure to the Antarctic, in
addition to seven members of the Expedition party who joined the
Terra Nova, more equipment was taken on board an already overloaded ship. This included nineteen ponies, thirty-three dogs, and
the three motor sledges packed in huge crates measuring 16′ × 3′ ×
4′, one being placed either side of the main hatch, while the third
was tethered across the back of the poop. Indeed, the ship was so
overloaded that on the morning of departure there was no deck
visible as all deck space had been taken up with Expedition equipment.[117]

As usual Scott was solicitous to recognise the help and personal
kindness which he had experienced in Cardiff, one source of which
was Alderman John Chappell, for whom Scott had come to form a
high regard during the preparations for the departure of the
Expedition from Cardiff. 'We . . . shall take pleasant memories of
Cardiff and the Lord Mayor of 1910'.[118]

The *Terra Nova* departed Lyttleton on 26 November and put in
briefly at Port Chalmers the deep water port of Dunedin to complete
her coaling before setting out for the Antarctic. Scott, accompanied
by P.O. Edgar Evans, travelled by train from Lyttleton to join the
ship at Port Chalmers. Evans had come within a hair's breadth of
being dismissed from the Expedition after he fell into the water in a
drunken state while attempting to board the *Terra Nova* in Lyttleton, but after constant entreaties persuaded Scott to keep him in the
party. In Port Chalmers, in addition to its full complement of coal,
an extra 30 tons of coal in sacks was stored on deck to put further
strain on an already seriously overloaded ship.[119]

On 29 November, the British Antarctic Expedition (1910) aboard
the *Terra Nova*, now some six weeks behind schedule, to a repeat of
the earlier farewells from Cardiff and more recently from Lyttleton,
at last set out for the Antarctic in its dangerously overloaded state.
And as Tryggve Gran, the Expedition's Norwegian ski expert put it,
if the ship 'was deep laden on leaving England, she was ready to sink
after departing from Port Chalmers'.[120]

Within two days of leaving the calm of Port Chalmers the *Terra
Nova* ran into a gale which turned into a violent storm for which the

southern seas are notorious, achieving a storm force of 11 out of 12 on the Beaufort scale. The *Terra Nova* was at the mercy of the storm for some thirty-six hours before it blew itself out on the morning of 3 December. During that period a good deal of damage was done to the ship such that she might even have capsized.[121]

In a New Year message to Daniel Radcliffe written at sea on 1 January 1911, Lt. Evans reflected on the progress since departing New Zealand in which he provided his personal account of the storm of 1–2 December and of its effects upon an overloaded boat.

' . . . in a very few days we shall be cut off from Politics and civilisation for a year. We embarked our Ponies and Dogs at Lyttleton, New Zealand on November 25th [1910] and left on the following day for the South. Can you imagine the "Terra Nova" with a deck cargo of 3 motor sledges, 33 dogs, 19 ponies, 30 Tons of Coal, 2500 gallons of petrol and some tons of pony fodder, and petroleum. We also carried 162 frozen sheep and 3 Bullocks in our ice house. As bad luck would have it we encountered a gale in 53° South and had a rotten time.

In our deeply laden condition we shipped a great deal of water and 40 feet of our bulwarks were washed away. We were hove to under lower tops'ls for 3 days. On the 2nd day two of the ponies died and one dog was killed, we lost 150 gallons of petrol and our pumps choked. We had a devil of a job clearing them. I haven't time to write you the details of all that has been done, but I shall be able to tell you when I return to Cardiff in 1912 I hope.

We entered the pack ice on Dec. 9th in Lat. 64°S and spent a happy Xmas altho' beset with ice. We got through into the open sea on Dec. 30th and sighted the big Mountain of Victoria Land on New Years' Eve.

Will you remember me very kindly to all my friends at that corner table'.[122]

Three days later the *Terra Nova* made fast at Cape Evans, so named by Scott after Lt. Evans, his second-in-command. The *Terra Nova* was unloaded and the base camp was established at Cape Evans, by the middle of January after which, before the end of the month, the southern or Polar party began its principal winter task of laying supply depots in preparation for an assault on the South Pole some time at the beginning of the Antarctic summer in September/October 1911.

Concurrently with the start of the depot laying journeys two parties departed Cape Evans in the *Terra Nova*, one of which was to be landed at King Edward VII Land at one end of the Great Ice Barrier,

[handwritten marginal note:] not true, only one party of 6 men

some 400 miles due east of Cape Evans, where the eastern party,
under Lt. Campbell, was to spend the winter on scientific work in
the unexplored region; the other party was to be landed some 400
miles north-east of Cape Evans as the *Terra Nova* returned to New
Zealand for the duration of the Antarctic winter.

In the Bay of Whales near King Edward VII Land on 3 February
1911, the *Terra Nova* encountered the *Fram*, the expedition ship of
the Norwegian Roald Amundsen who, it transpired, had arrived on
15 January and had established his base camp high on the ice barrier
some 60 miles further south than Hut Point. Instead of returning
immediately to New Zealand, the *Terra Nova* back-tracked to Cape
Evans where, on 8 February, Lt. Campbell left a message detailing
Amundsen's whereabouts to await Scott's return from his depot
journey. Now, with coal stocks at a seriously low level and the
Antarctic winter fast closing in the *Terra Nova* steamed north
towards New Zealand, hurriedly depositing the two parties, now
amalgamated under the command of Lt. Campbell, on the tip of
Cape Adare in the already explored region of South Victoria Land.

Scott's main depot laying journey during the winter of 1911 did
not progress as well as had been anticipated and gave cause for concern for the ultimate success of his Expedition. It became apparent
that the achievement on 17 February of Scott's furthest position
South, 79° 28½ S, where One Ton Depot was established, had taken
much longer than was desirable. This was mainly because the
ponies favoured by Scott were too slow and proved quite unsuitable
for Antarctic conditions such that Scott's party had taken twenty-
four days to reach this latitude. Amundsen, by contrast, relying
exclusively on dogs for transport in his depot laying preparations,
had reached a point slightly further South (80°S) and had returned to
his base camp in a mere five days.[123] Scott's problems were more
than compounded when on his return from One Ton Camp and having reached Safety Camp on 22 February—about a mile and a half
from his base at Hut Point—he received Lt. Campbell's intelligence
that Amundsen had established his base at the Bay of Whales.

By the middle of May all members of the Polar section of the
British Antarctic Expedition had assembled in their headquarters at
Cape Evans for the duration of the most severe part of the Antarctic
winter during which they made final preparations for Scott's assault
on the South Pole in the summer months of October to February
1911–12.[124] Amundsen intended to make his attempt on the Pole at
the same time and aimed to return to his base camp by the end of

January 1912, though Scott, unaccountably, gave his party at Cape Evans the date of 27 March as the latest time when they might expect his return. Scott seems to have been reconciled to a late return from the Pole and the prospect of remaining a further year in the Antarctic. He said as much in a letter he wrote to Daniel Radcliffe sent from Dunedin in February 1911, but written before he embarked on his depot laying expedition in January. 'If the Terra Nova is a year late in reaching Cardiff Docks you must blame the Antarctic climate . . . You must give my kind regards to our Cardiff friends whose sympathy I shall not readily forget'.[125]

'Teddy' Evans, too, seems to have become half resigned to another winter in the Antarctic, when he wrote in September 1911 to both Daniel Radcliffe and Percy Lewis, anticipating a push for the Pole in November. He informed Radcliffe, 'I am just writing you a little note in case we do not get back from the South in time to leave in the 'Terra Nova' next March. It is a case of even chances I think! . . . The sun has only just returned and sledging will be very unpleasant until November—I expect I shall get temperatures down to 60° below zero. The coldest we have had this winter was 79° below zero.' Evans commented on the trials of establishing One Ton Depot, 'We lost several ponies as they couldn't stand blizzards. 3 were drowned through the ice breaking up suddenly, but we have 10 left.

I suppose you have heard about the Norwegian expedition turning up here having a go at the Pole—I hope the best man may win.' And again he remembered his Cardiff friends, 'By jove, Dan, I have many many times wished myself at your little Table at the Exchange Restaurant with Bill Tatem, Joe Frazer and all those damn good chaps'.[126]

Some of these thoughts were echoed in his letter to Percy Lewis. 'In case we do not get back from our forthcoming sledge journey to the South I am writing you a short letter to say that I often think of you and your dear family. I mean "by not getting back" that we may not return here till late March by which time the *Terra Nova* will have sailed northward to avoid being frozen in . . . We burn nothing in our stoves but Crown Patent Fuel. Once our men got used to it they had no use for anything else. It knocks spots off coal down here. We built our stable wall of the blocks . . . ' He ends somewhat wistfully, 'Dear old Cardiff seems so close'.[127] In a letter to another, unidentified, Cardiff friend, probably Percy Lewis, Evans states simply that 'I leave here on October 22 with the two motor sledges and the heavier weights for the South'.[128]

Scott and Amundsen from points about 400 miles apart, both set out for the South Pole within a few days of each other; Amundsen on 10 October and Scott on 1 November 1911. Amundsen, faithful to his Nordic experience, relied exclusively on dogs to haul his sledges and equipment. Scott opted for a combination of motor sledges and ponies—which had already proved quite unsuitable for Antarctic conditions—and relied upon man-hauling his sledges for the final assault on the Pole. In the event Amundsen claimed the Pole on 15 December 1911. He returned to his base camp at the Bay of Whales by 5 February 1912 and almost immediately departed the Antarctic in the *Fram* bound for New Zealand where he arrived at the beginning of March to announce that he had gained the Pole for Norway.

Scott meanwhile by 4 January was still 150 miles from the Pole. It was here that Scott and his four companions bade farewell to their main support party led by Lt. Evans. On the return of the support party to Cape Evans, Lt. Evans contracted scurvy and was fortunate to be the subject of an heroic rescue by his two companions, Chief Stoker William Lashly and P.O. Crean.[129] Lt. Evans remained at Cape Evans until the *Terra Nova* returned to the Antarctic for a second time, expecting to pick up Scott and return with the whole Expeditionary party. In their absence, 'Teddy' Evans himself returned to New Zealand to recuperate and it was only on his arrival there that he learned of Amundsen's triumph and actually met him. As for Scott, it was some twelve months before the news of his death became public knowledge.

Scott and his companions, Dr. Edward Wilson, Capt. Lawrence Oates, Lt. H.R. Bowers and P.O. 'Taffy' Edgar Evans, reached the Pole on 17 January 1912, thirty-four days after Amundsen, and in the face of the severe Antarctic winter perished on their return journey in February and March within a few miles of the safety of One Ton Camp.

Lt. Evans returned to the United Kingdom in 1912 for the duration of the Antarctic winter where he attended to business affairs at the headquarters of the Antarctic Expedition in London. The Cardiff connexion was maintained. Evans and his wife Hilda came to Cardiff to see their friends and stayed in June 1912 with the Gethin Lewises and their son Percy at 'Nythfa', 20 Cathedral Road. Lt. Evans's stay in Cathedral Road coincided with an extended visit to Cardiff by King George V and Queen Mary, during which he and his wife were invited by the city authorities to be guests at the various ceremonies connected with the royal visit. There he was able to enjoy the company of Cardiff friends, including supporters of the Antarctic Expedition, such as W.J. Tatem, Daniel Radcliffe,

J.S. Fraser, Gethin Lewis and other city worthies. One evening Evans was called aboard the Royal Yacht where he would have had the opportunity to inform the King of the known progress of the Antarctic Expedition. Before Evans left the yacht King George, rather exceptionally, took it upon himself to promote the young lieutenant to the rank of Lt. Commander to make him the youngest officer of that rank in the Royal Navy.[130]

Lt. Commander Evans returned to New Zealand by November 1912 to take command of the *Terra Nova* for the relief expedition. In a letter, probably addressed to Percy Lewis, on 27 November he wrote to say that they were leaving for the Antarctic on 14 December, and 'we hope to bring back Capt. Scott and the members of the Expedition safely back here by March 15' [1913].[131] I will write to you from the Antarctic, and let you know how we get on, so expect to hear from me again by May 1'. Meanwhile in Britain, Roald Amundsen had arrived in London to begin a series of lectures, 'How I reached the Pole', one of which he delivered in the Park Hall in Cardiff on 3 December 1912. The *Western Mail* reported that the Lord Major 'conveyed to the Explorer the welcome of the City which had done a great deal in financing Scott's Expedition on the *Terra Nova*'.[132] On the following day Amundsen repeated the performance in Newport.

The *Terra Nova* departed New Zealand on 15 December and reached Cape Evans on 18 January 1913. When the ship arrived it was the occasion on which Commander Evans first learned of the death of Capt. Scott and the Polar party. The occasion was recorded in the Log of the *Terra Nova*, 'Found here 19 men under Lieut. V.L.A. Campbell R.N. (in good health) who informed us that Capt. Scott and the advance party reached the South Pole on Jan. 18th 1912 and were all lost on the return journey dying from exposure and want'.[133]

With the ice closing in with the onset of the Antarctic winter all haste was made to clear up what remained of the Expedition at Cape Evans and the full party returned to New Zealand, with Commander Evans in overall command. On the return to New Zealand, Francis Drake, Secretary to the Expedition, attended to the considerable correspondence which had accumulated awaiting Scott's arrival. One such letter was from Daniel Radcliffe who had written to Scott in October 1911—just about the time that Scott set out in earnest for the South Pole—to express his good wishes for the Polar journey and hoping this letter would reach him, 'finding you quite well after your arduous journeys in the southern regions, and I hope you have been successful'.[134] Drake returned the letter to Radcliffe from the *Terra Nova* in January 1913. 'Herewith your letter to Captain Scott, which was unable to be delivered owing to his sad death. Please excuse such a short notice. You will realise how busy I am.'

In a letter of 6 February written 'at sea' before the *Terra Nova* reached New Zealand Commander Evans informed Percy Lewis, 'I have ordered the *Terra Nova* to Cardiff so that the real friends of the Expedition, those men who did *most* generously give, can see the little ship that carried their hopes for the honourable execution of a difficult mission . . . Goodbye till May 1st' [1913].[135]

News of the Antarctic tragedy was cabled to London from New Zealand on 10 February 1913, and by the time the *Terra Nova* docked at Lyttleton two days later, the tragic news was known throughout the world. Kathleen Scott was aboard a passenger liner bound for New Zealand where she was expecting to meet her husband after the Expedition had been relieved, when on 19 February she received the news of Scott's death from the Captain of the liner.

The news of the deaths of Scott and his companions hit the front pages of Britain's newspapers of Tuesday, 11 February 1913 and daily for the rest of that week the tragedy was the principal feature in the *Western Mail*. The immediate response of the Cardiff Docksmen was to accord their respect to the memory of Captain Scott by draping with the Union Jack and black crepe Richard Short's painting of the *Terra Nova* which occupied pride of place in the Library of the Exchange Building.[136] The Lord Mayor approached Daniel Radcliffe to discuss the possibilities of erecting a memorial to Scott in Cathays Park and of holding a memorial service on 29 March, the anniversary of Scott's death.[137] In the event, however, a service of remembrance was held in St. John's Church at the first opportunity on the following Sunday, 16 February. [138]

At a meeting of Cardiff City Council on 18 February, attended by representatives of the Docks community, a joint Council/Docks appeal committee was established, chaired by the Lord Mayor, with Daniel Radcliffe elected to serve as Treasurer. A few days later, on 22 February, the joint committee met to draft the text of a letter of appeal. Before proceeding the committee was informed that Daniel Radcliffe had been invited by Sir Edward Speyer, Treasurer of the Committee of the British Antarctic Expedition (1910) to become an additional member of the Committee and had been asked 'if your firm will act as agents and representatives of the Expedition at Cardiff', when the *Terra Nova* returned.[139]

The appeal committee had no doubt that the Cardiff connexion had been crucial in ensuring the viability of the Antarctic Expedition and emphasis was given to this belief in the letter of appeal. In the initial draft Cardiffians were reminded that Cardiff's part in the Expedition was such that the enterprise 'was, perhaps to a greater extent than the general public realise, in reality a <u>Welsh</u> Antarctic Expedition'. On reflection some may have expressed doubts as to the wisdom of making such an assertion and the final version was modified to read, 'the Antarctic Expedition was, perhaps to a greater extent than the general public realise, an enterprise in which Wales was particularly interested, as the citizens of Cardiff not only subscribed very generously to the funds of the Expedition, but Cardiff was the Port from which these gallant men set out. Cardiff is the Port to which the Terra Nova will return'.[140]

The appeal committee commissioned the printing of 5,000 copies of the letter of appeal and arranged that they should be delivered to every house-hold in the principal residential streets of the city. At the same time, the *Western Mail* and the *South Wales Daily News* of 24 February carried the text of the letter of appeal. High hopes were entertained of a generous response to the appeal, especially from the Cardiff Chamber of Commerce whose membership stood at about 400.[141]

Although Daniel Radcliffe assumed leadership of the fund raising efforts for the Memorial Appeal among the Docks community, no one played a similar role on behalf of the civic authorities. Early on Radcliffe appeared confident of a successful response to the appeal and wrote to John Wheatley, the Town Clerk, in March, 'we are working hard down here, and will let you know as soon as possible as to calling a meeting of the Committee'.[142]

By early May the sum subscribed to the Scott Memorial Appeal, as Radcliffe informed the Memorial Appeal Committee, was £328.2s.0d., most of which sum had been donated by members of the Docks community, while a mere £78.4s.6d. had been received from donations by way of the Lord Mayor. The portents for the success of the appeal were distinctly unfavourable even though Radcliffe ventured the hope that it might eventually reach £1,000.[143]

Commander Evans arrived back in Britain in April, the victim of personal tragedy earlier in the year. While returning from New Zealand with his wife aboard a P and O liner ahead of the *Terra Nova*, Hilda Evans developed peritonitis and died on board ship in the

Mediterranean. Evans buried his wife in Toulon from whence he travelled back to Britain.[144]

In advance of the arrival of the *Terra Nova* in Cardiff, 'Teddy' Evans worked at the London headquarters of the British Antarctic Expedition to try to get into shape the business affairs of the Expedition.[145] Soon after his return Evans turned for support to his old Cardiff friends, the Gethin Lewises of Cathedral Road, with whom he stayed for a few days at the beginning of May. Commander Evans had made a point of bringing back to Britain the remaining personal effects of his namesake, Petty Officer 'Taffy' Evans from Swansea. While staying in Cathedral Road in May, Evans and his friend Percy Lewis, motored down to Swansea to visit Mrs. Evans to hand over the diary and pocket book of her late husband.[146] When Commander Evans came to Cardiff ahead of the *Terra Nova's* anticipated arrival, he stayed for a short while with his old friend Daniel Radcliffe before retiring to Cathedral Road to await the *Terra Nova's* return to Cardiff, as Scott had promised.

All plans for the welcome of the *Terra Nova* and her crew, as well as the arrangements for the discharge of her stores, equipment, scientific specimens, and for the general winding up of the ship's affairs were taken in hand by Daniel Radcliffe, now the official agent of the British Antarctic Committee (1910) in Cardiff.

The *Terra Nova* arrived off the Scilly Isles where on Thursday, 12 June, she was boarded by Commander Evans for her return to Cardiff on Saturday.[147] Kathleen, now Lady Scott, an honour conferred upon her personally by the King, came down to Cardiff to welcome home the officers and crew of her husband's ship. She travelled by train to Newport on Friday with her young son Peter, where they stayed as guests of Mr. and Mrs. Jestyn Williams of 'Brynderwen', Summerhill Avenue, Maindee.[148]

A number of other close relatives of members of the British Antarctic Expedition came down to Cardiff on Friday to await the return of the *Terra Nova*, including Oriana, widow of Dr. Edward Wilson, who stayed at the Royal Hotel.[149]

On Saturday morning, 14 June 1913 shortly before 11 a.m. Lady Scott and young Peter arrived at the Pier Head, Cardiff Docks, having been driven by motor car from Newport by their host Mr. Jestyn Williams. The *Terra Nova* had lain at anchor off Flatholm since early that morning and at the request of Lady Scott the tug *Nelson* was reserved to carry her and her young son together with a small party of close friends, which included Mrs. Wilson, out to the vessel to

This card was originally printed by E. Davies & Co. of Cardiff on the return of the *Terra Nova* in 1913.

enable them to share a private reunion away from the glare of publicity. Within the hour Daniel Radcliffe, the ex-Mayor John Chappell and other prominent Cardiff friends of the Expedition were ferried out to the *Terra Nova* aboard the tug *Mercedes* to pay their respects to the ship's personnel.[150]

The *Terra Nova* weighed anchor at about 12.30 p.m. and as she came into view of the spectators on the shore it was observed that the flag bearing the arms of the City of Cardiff was flying from the foremast while the flag bearing the Welsh Dragon was hoisted on the mainmast. *The Times* reported that 'Lady Scott walked the deck of the vessel inspecting the many objects of interest shown her by the officers, while little Peter wandered all over the ship . . . rockets were fired and cheering came from hundreds of school-children on the banks. Commander Evans handed his white peaked cap to Peter Scott, and at his behest the boy acknowledged the cheers'.[151]

A memorial service was held on Sunday morning in the Docks Parish Church presided over by the Bishop of Llandaff. In the afternoon special trains were laid on to conduct the thousands of spectators expected to want to see the ship in Cardiff Docks and it was estimated that some 60,000 sightseers took the opportunity to do so.[152]

On Monday at noon proceedings at the Cardiff Exchange were suspended to enable the members to welcome the officers and crew of the *Terra Nova* on the occasion of their return to Cardiff, and especially to pay their respects to the bereaved Mrs. Edward Wilson and Mrs. Edgar Evans who were present. In his address of thanks to the Cardiff Docksmen for their hospitality at this reception, Commander Evans took advantage of the occasion to remind all present that 'it was in Cardiff that Captain Scott's expedition was made possible . . . ' The high point of the day was a dinner in the evening at the Royal Hotel, almost exactly three years to the day on which the Expedition had departed Cardiff in search of the South Pole. The dinner was an occasion for renewing old friendships and for expressing thanks to the citizens of Cardiff for ensuring that the Expedition set out for the Antarctic. Commander Evans repeated his remarks made at the Exchange earlier in the day that it was fitting that they should have come back to Cardiff 'because it was Cardiff that had made the Expedition possible'. Evans made public the important role played by the *Western Mail* in ensuring maximum publicity for the Expedition, and of the staff of the newspaper he paid particular thanks to W.E. Davies, the Editor, for providing him with valuable assistance, especially for his advice as to whom to canvass for funds. 'To those representatives of the *Western Mail* and to Mr. William Davies I say "Thank you", although I know Mr. Davies will hate me for saying so'.

Commander Evans announced that the Welsh Flag was to be given to the National Museum of Wales; the City flag was presented to the City authorities, and the White Ensign which had flown throughout the voyage of the *Terra Nova* was offered as a gift to Daniel Radcliffe, who, as the *Western Mail* reporter pointed out had done so much for the Expedition, 'more, possibly than any other man in the Kingdom'.[153] The reporter might have added that Radcliffe was renowned for having taken a close personal interest in the well-being of the members of the Expeditionary party. A few days after the *Terra Nova* docked in Cardiff Radcliffe received a letter of thanks for his efforts from Murray Levick, one of the two naval surgeons on the Antarctic Expedition, which reflected these sentiments.[154] 'You more than anyone else have helped to make both our visits to Cardiff, a pleasant memory which we will always retain, and it is very difficult for us to express to you our appreciation of all you have done for us, and of you yourself as a real good sort: the last being the more important.

Another thing is, it is a source of some pride to me to think that each time we were in Cardiff, I slept under your roof.'

Before June was out Messrs Bowring Brothers took up their option of repurchasing the *Terra Nova* for about £5,000. The crew of the *Terra Nova* were paid off in Cardiff and it was generally expected that the ship would remain in Cardiff Docks for about three weeks while she was discharged of the Expedition equipment, stores and geological specimens, most of which were bound for the British Museum. At the end of her period in Cardiff Docks the *Terra Nova* was scheduled to return to her former whaling duties in the northern seas off Newfoundland.[155]

While the *Terra Nova* was being prepared in Cardiff for her return to northern waters Commander Evans made a short visit to London to deliver some lectures on the recent Antarctic Expedition, at one of which in the Queen's Hall, Sir Ernest Shackleton alluded to the fact, hitherto known to but a few, that in the summer of 1909, the then Lt. Evans was actively preparing to launch his own Expedition to the Antarctic.

Now that Commander Evans's earlier Antarctic plans had become public knowledge, as a prelude to a lecture by Evans in Cardiff in early July, W.E. Davies, in an article in the *Western Mail*, took it upon himself to confirm Shackleton's remarks and to ensure that Evans was accorded credit for abandoning his own Antarctic plans and for having put himself and the contacts which he had established in Cardiff at the disposal of Captain Scott.[156]

The revelations by the editor of the *Western Mail* prompted speculation that Commander Evans might use the occasion of his lecture to the Cardiff Naturalists' Society to announce that he had decided to proceed to lead his own expedition, perhaps even an all-Welsh expedition, to the Antarctic.[157] In the event no such announcement was forthcoming and the audience in the Park Hall was treated to an exciting lecture enhanced by spectacular still and moving pictures taken by Herbert Ponting, the camera artist engaged by the British Antarctic Expedition. Daniel Radcliffe had ensured that Lashly and Crean, who had saved Commander Evans's life in the Antarctic, were present at the lecture so that they might receive public recognition for their brave deeds. Soon after the well attended and successful lecture the Cardiff Naturalists' Society contributed a substantial sum to Commander Evans to help towards meeting the outstanding costs of the Antarctic Expedition.[158]

Speculation as to Commander Evans's future Antarctic career was premature since he had already arranged to go on half pay from the Royal Navy and he had planned almost immediately after his Cardiff lecture to take advantage of a lecture tour of the United States and Canada in the summer and autumn of 1913. He saw this as an opportunity to take stock of his future, an experience from which he returned convinced that he should proceed with his career in the Royal Navy. In his travels in North America Evans was accompanied by his Cardiff friend, Percy Lewis, whose friendship he acknowledged to be a source of inspiration over the years.[159]

On the morning of July 1 the *Terra Nova* was opened for inspection by the public on payment of a fee of 1s per adult and 6d for a child, such that by the end of the week it was reported that £25 had been collected, though it was unclear whether the monies raised would go towards meeting the debts of the British Antarctic Expedition (1910) or to the Cardiff Memorial Appeal.[160] In fact, donations to the Scott Memorial Appeal had all but dried up by early May 1913 and the portents for further contributions were unfavourable.

The disappointing response to the Scott Memorial Appeal was doubtless common knowledge among establishment figures in both

Docks and Civic communities. However, in the absence of any announcements as to what was envisaged as a suitable memorial to Scott and of his connexion with Cardiff, early in July 1913 just before the *Terra Nova* was expected to depart the City, Mr. F.C. Bowring, Chairman of Bowring Brothers of Liverpool and currently prospective Liberal Parliamentary candidate for Cardiff, agreed to a request by Councillor G.F. Forsdike of the Parks Committee to donate the figurehead of the *Terra Nova* to the City of Cardiff as a memorial to Captain Scott which might be displayed on a site at the southern end of Roath Park lake.[161]

Almost coincident with this initiative by Councillor Forsdike it became apparent that the *Terra Nova* would remain in Cardiff Docks for a few weeks longer than had been anticipated. The whaling season did not begin until September before which the *Terra Nova* underwent a re-fit in Cardiff Docks, from which eventually she departed with no ceremony—and without her figurehead—early in the evening of 15 August 1913.[162]

Contributions to the Scott Memorial Fund which had been non-existent since May 1913 received a welcome boost in November by way of a donation of £100 from Lord Merthyr on behalf of the Cardiff Railway Company, which served to increase the Appeal funds to about £430.[163] This addition to the Memorial Fund was made less than a fortnight before the scheduled unveiling of the *Terra Nova* figurehead at Roath Park lake, when public attention was bound to turn to the current state of the official Scott Memorial Fund.

The figurehead of the *Terra Nova* was formally presented to the City of Cardiff by Mr. F.C. Bowring at a ceremony at the southern end of Roath Park on 8 December 1913. He suggested that the *Terra Nova*, through her ownership and her Welsh commander, might be looked upon as a Cardiff vessel. If left to the elements the life of the wooden figurehead by its very nature was bound to be of limited duration, and at the end of his speech Mr. Bowring announced that he would be prepared to erect, at his own expense, a memorial in the form of a clock tower near to the site of the figurehead which would serve as a permanent reminder of Scott and his companions and of the unique connexion between Cardiff and the British Antarctic Expedition (1910).[164]

In performing the task of unveiling the figurehead Commander Evans paid tribute to the support which the Expedition had received from Cardiff and was glad to remind all present that 'had it not been for Cardiff's generosity the Expedition would not have sailed in 1910'.[165]

The offer of a Clock Tower by Mr. F.C. Bowring to the memory of Scott at the unveiling of the figurehead of the *Terra Nova* obliged some sort of statement concerning the affairs of the official Memorial Appeal Fund, which emerged by way of the speech of thanks by the Lord Mayor Alderman James Robinson to Mr. Bowring for his generous gifts to the City, supplemented by a statement by Councillor G.F. Forsdike on behalf of the Scott Memorial Committee.

The assembled were afforded the uninspiring news that sufficient funds had been donated to the Scott Memorial Fund to endow a Memorial Bed in the Royal Hamadryad Hospital in the Docks while hope was expressed that in due course a Memorial Tablet might be erected in the City Hall to commemorate Scott—clearly not the sort of recognition for Scott and his connexion with Cardiff which had been envisaged at the launch of the Memorial Appeal in February 1913. That evening, following the ceremonies at Roath Park Lake, the citizens of Cardiff were given an opportunity to hear again Commander Evans's lecture on the Antarctic Expedition and with the accompaniment of Herbert Ponting's magnificent photographs to be reminded of the hazards faced by Scott and his companions.[166]

The plans for the Scott Memorial as announced at the ceremonies at Roath Park Lake were both a consequence of the disappointing response to the Appeal Fund and a manifestation of the political differences which had developed between the Docks and the Civic communities arising from the growth in the prosperity and influence of the Port of Cardiff in recent years.[167] Differences between the two communities had been obscured in the spirit of co-operation which had attended the preparations for the voyage of the *Terra Nova*. They now re-surfaced over the issue as to where and with whom responsibility lay for the failure of the Scott Memorial Appeal.

It would seem that the Docksmen took the view that since the success of the Cardiff connexion with the British Antarctic Expedition (1910) was based upon the support which had been afforded to the enterprise by the Docks community—an association which had brought great publicity and prestige to Cardiff and had reflected well on the City Council—it was now properly the turn of the Civic authorities to take the lead in organising and contributing a fitting Memorial to Scott. In fact, throughout the duration of the Memorial Appeal, contributions by way of the Civic authorities were minimal.

Thus by the end of 1913, if not earlier, frustrated at the apparent

Clock Tower, Roath Park Lake.
Photograph by Bob Watkins

Plaque affixed to the clock tower,
Roath Park Lake.
Photographed by Bob Watkins.

lack of commitment by the Civic authorities to the creation of a suitable memorial to Scott, the representatives of the Docksmen on the Committee of the Scott Memorial Appeal—the Treasurer of which was Daniel Radcliffe—employed their influence to ensure that since the bulk of the Appeal Funds had originated from within the Docks community the main priority should be the establishment of a Memorial which both reflected the unique association of the Docks community with the Scott Expedition and redounded to its benefit. Consequently, in the name of the Appeal Committee, it was agreed to endow a Memorial Bed in the Royal Hamadryad Hospital.[168] Any balance remaining in the fund, effectively the money collected by way of the Civic authorities, was assigned to the creation of a Scott Memorial Tablet for display in the City Hall. In the event, while the aspirations of the Docks community were satisfied with the establishment in the summer of 1914 of what came to be known as the 'Terra Nova' Bed, a further two years elapsed before the creation of a Scott Memorial Tablet was achieved.

The outbreak of war in the summer of 1914 afforded opportunities for delay and even neglect of the completion of the Memorial Tablet. However, as in most matters concerning Cardiff and the British Antarctic Expedition, the completion of the Memorial Tablet was achieved as a result of the efforts of Daniel Radcliffe—ably supported on this occasion by J.L. Wheatley, the Town Clerk and Secretary to the Memorial Appeal Committee—who supplied the drive and determination to ensure that the Civic authorities fulfilled their obligation to the memory of Captain Scott.

The poor response to the Memorial Appeal prevented the engage· ment of a well-known or even experienced sculptor to create the Memorial Tablet. Until such time as an artist could be commissioned to carry out the work J.L. Wheatley took what steps he was able to assemble background information about Scott which might be of benefit to whomsoever eventually was appointed to carry out the project. He took initiatives to contact those closest to Scott, such as Commander Evans and Scott's two sisters, but above all it was Kathleen Scott who attended to his queries with commendable patience.

By the end of June 1914 Wheatley was in a position to inform Lady Scott and Commander Evans of the firm intention of the Scott Memorial Committee to arrange for the creation of a Memorial Tablet to Scott which would be erected in the City Hall. In a letter to Lady Scott, Wheatley explained that ' . . . we are anxious to put up something in our Civic Buildings which includes the connection between the late Captain Scott of the 'Terra Nova' and the City . . . '[169] For his part Commander Evans was happy to confirm the details of two queries posed by Wheatley. He reassured Wheatley as to the date of Scott's death, 'The <u>date</u> has been accepted as 29 March—so you need have no fear on that subject', and further that the wooden cross erected to the memory of Scott and his companions at Observation Point at McMurdo Sound did indeed carry the inscription, 'To serve, to seek, to find, and not to yield'.[170]

Wheatley betrayed his ignorance of the terrain of the Antarctic when he sought from Lady Scott her views as to suitable Antarctic flora which might be depicted on the Memorial plaque, to which rather tiresome request she replied in the courteous manner characteristic of her correspondence.

'In answer to your letter I don't think the edilweis grows in the antarctic. Capt. Scott's crest was a Stag's head with the motto, "Ready, aye, ready".

I think the best photograph of him is the one sold on the book-

Scott Memorial Tablet, City Hall, Cardiff.
By Permission of Cardiff City Council

stalls for 6d. I could, however, send you others if this one is not liked'.[171]

A few days later Lady Scott sent Wheatley photographs of both Scott and the *Terra Nova* for possible use by the artist.[172]

In his endeavours to obtain material, Miss G.M. Scott, the explorer's younger sister, provided valuable details about her brother's early career, in addition to which she arranged for her sister, Mrs. K.M. Brownlow, to send on loan the flag which Scott had used on his sledge, which, she informed him, had been hand-made by Scott's mother according to a design of Sir Clements Markham, Scott's mentor.[173]

It was not until November 1914 that J.L. Wheatley was in a position to inform Daniel Radcliffe that he had managed to secure the services of a young sculptor, W.W. Wagstaffe, said to be an artist of great promise, who was prepared to accept the commission to sculpt and produce the Scott Memorial Tablet for the sum of the balance of the Memorial Fund which stood at £72.14s.2d. including the interest to the end of the year. It was agreed that payment for this commission which, Wagstaffe stressed, he had undertaken at great financial sacrifice to himself, would be in three equal instalments of £24. Wheatley was acutely aware that the Memorial Committee was fortunate in securing the services of this young man, since 'it would have been quite impossible to get the work done by the older established sculptors for treble that amount . . . The Design is the outcome of much thought on my part and after perusing the Volumes of "Scott's Last Expedition", and I believe it represents accurately the character of the man and the physical nature of his great and glorious enterprise and achievement'.[174]

It was proposed that the Memorial Tablet should be sculpted in a style to harmonise with the existing Tablet erected in honour of the former City M.P., Sir Edward Reed, which adorned the left-hand wall, half-way up the main staircase in the City Hall. The Scott Memorial was to be erected on the right-hand wall opposite.[175]

Though extremely appreciative of Wheatley's efforts in securing the commission of a fitting Memorial to Captain Scott, Radcliffe's reply to Wheatley's proposals provide an illuminating insight into his bitter disappointment at the outcome of the Memorial Appeal and especially at the apathetic attitude displayed by the leaders of the Cardiff City Council towards the whole project: 'Surely Alderman Thomas has been able to get more subscriptions. We had six Aldermen and Town Councillors on the Committee, none of whom have given a penny. Only Alderman Thomas has subscribed out of the seven. I was under the impression Alderman Thomas was going to collect certain sums amongst them to enlarge the fund. I quite approve of all you have done . . .'[176]

Formal approval of the project, including the conditions of Wagstaffe's commission, and the details of the planned site for the Memorial in the City Hall, was given initially at a meeting of the Property and Markets Committee in December and endorsed by the full Council at the end of January 1915.[177]

Now secure in his commission, Wagstaffe went ahead with creating the Scott Memorial Tablet in his London studios in Justice Walk, Chelsea. Wheatley for his part continued to glean information as to Scott's life and career. Of two such enquiries, both made early in February 1915, one sought to establish the correct date of Scott's birth in anticipation of its inclusion on the Memorial. Lady Scott was able to confirm Scott's birth date as 6 June 1868 with characteristic courtesy, 'I am glad to be able to give you any information'.[178] The second enquiry was framed to elicit the views of Lady Scott as to the propriety of using the appellation 'Sir' upon the inscription of the Memorial Plaque. This enquiry fortunately coincided with a brief visit by Lady Scott to London from Alsace where she was working in a French military hospital. She attended to the enquiry immediately, 'Captain Scott was given the posthumous decoration of K.C.B. I should certainly not put Sir R.F. Scott on the tablet, as he was never known by that title. I don't know how the tablet reads but Knight Commander of the Bath was given when news of his death reached this country'.[179] It was in advance of Lady Scott's visit to London a few weeks later at the beginning of April 1915 which prompted her sister-in-law, Mrs. K.M. Brownlow, to ask Wheatley for the return of Scott's sledging flag which had been in his care for some months. On the occasion of its return Wheatley was able to inform her that a representation of the flag would appear on the Memorial.[180]

The completion of the Scott Memorial suffered a number of delays. Wagstaffe had entertained high hopes of fulfilling his commission by mid-July 1915. In June, on the occasion of the date for the third and final instalment of his fee, he asked Wheatley for £60 to meet unexpected expenses arising from the costs of the bronze foundry but received £25.0s.1d. 'which sum' said Wheatley, 'exhausts the funds'.[181] Wagstaffe assured Wheatley that the tablet cost him £167.18s.10d. to produce, 'considerably more than I have received for it'.[182] The Tablet remained unfinished in November 1915.[183] This final delay arose because the foundry had been ordered temporarily to suspend its artistic work for the production of vital munitions.[184] The Tablet arrived in Cardiff at the end of January 1916 ready for erection in the City Hall, and was eventually fixed in place on the right-hand side of the Grand Staircase under the direction of the City Engineer, William Harpur, at the beginning of February.[185]

Because the Memorial Tablet had been completed at the height of the war none of the former members of the Antarctic Expedition nor those closest to Scott was available to unveil the Tablet. Quite quickly, however, Wheatley was able to secure the services of Major General Sir Francis Lloyd, Major General Commanding London District, to perform the unveiling ceremony. His appropriateness for the honour however seemed to extend little further than the coincidence that he was a high ranking officer and a Welshman.

Daniel Radcliffe found the invitation to Major General Sir Francis Lloyd acceptable, but felt obliged to remind the Town Clerk that the Memorial Tablet and the 'Terra Nova' Bed at the Hamadryad Hospital had been established out of the same fund, and suggested that Sir Francis Lloyd might be invited to open both memorials on the same day.[186] In communicating the request to Major General Lloyd the following day, Wheatley took the opportunity to explain the connexion between the two events: 'For your information, both Memorials are the result of one and the same Fund, the Mural Tablet in the City Hall was obtained out of the surplus, so that if you will be so considerate as to perform both ceremonies, you will afford much gratification to the subscribers'.[187]

Sir Francis Lloyd clearly had little idea of the significance of the connexion between Cardiff and the British Antarctic Expedition and in response to a request from Lloyd's A.D.C. for such information, Wheatley produced a 'briefing paper', to help him.

'It was from this Port that the Expedition sailed. The major portion of the expenses connected with the Expedition was obtained in this district and the 'Terra Nova' received all of its coal from here . . .

The practical interest shown by prominent citizens in this Expedition reflected great credit upon them as without their wholehearted co-operation it was very doubtful whether the Expedition could have been made'.[188]

Radcliffe made all arrangements with Major General Lloyd concerning his opening of the 'Terra Nova' bed. He put his motor car at

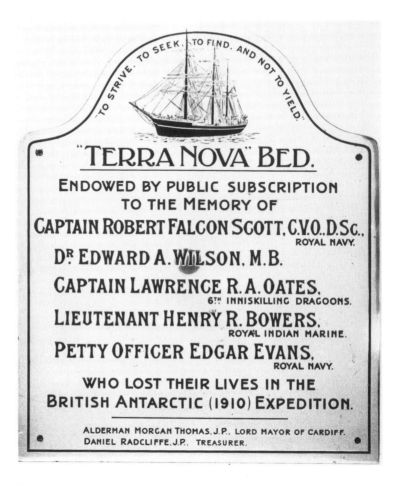

"TO STRIVE, TO SEEK, TO FIND, AND NOT TO YIELD."

"TERRA NOVA" BED.

ENDOWED BY PUBLIC SUBSCRIPTION TO THE MEMORY OF

CAPTAIN ROBERT FALCON SCOTT, C.V.O., D.Sc.,
ROYAL NAVY.

DR EDWARD A. WILSON, M.B.

CAPTAIN LAWRENCE R. A. OATES,
6TH INNISKILLING DRAGOONS.

LIEUTENANT HENRY R. BOWERS,
ROYAL INDIAN MARINE.

PETTY OFFICER EDGAR EVANS,
ROYAL NAVY.

WHO LOST THEIR LIVES IN THE BRITISH ANTARCTIC (1910) EXPEDITION.

ALDERMAN MORGAN THOMAS, J.P., LORD MAYOR OF CARDIFF.
DANIEL RADCLIFFE, J.P., TREASURER.

'Terra Nova' Bed Memorial Plaque, Royal Hamadryad Hospital, Cardiff (by kind permission of the South Glamorgan Area Health Authority).

the disposal of the General and undertook to convey him first to the Hamadryad Hospital and thence to the City Hall.[189] On the morning of 10 April 1916 Major General Lloyd, in the company of Daniel Radcliffe, his brother Henry, W.J. Tatem, Chairman of the Hamadryad Hospital, officially opened the 'Terra Nova' Bed, dedicated to the memory of Capt. Scott and his four companions who lost their lives on their return from the South Pole. With a fine sense of occasion which might well have been calculated to put the poor response to the Scott Memorial Appeal into a proper perspective, Daniel Radcliffe, on behalf of his brother and himself, presented the General with a cheque for £1,050 to dedicate a bed next to the 'Terra Nova' Bed, to the memory of Lt. Commander Henry Rennick, formerly lieutenant aboard the *Terra Nova* who lost his life in September 1914 when H.M.S. *Hogue* was sunk in action.[190]

The erection of the Clock Tower to the memory of Capt. Scott and his companions was, by contrast with the problems which had surrounded the creation of the two Memorials funded by public subscriptions, a straightforward affair. The Clock Tower was completed, and had become a prominent feature in Roath Park lake for more than a year before the 'Terra Nova' Bed and the Scott Memorial Tablet had been unveiled. The two Memorials funded by subscription failed to command anything like the same public attention as that attained by the Clock Tower which had been created as a result of the generosity of Mr. F.C. Bowring of Liverpool. In the circumstances, as far as many contemporaries were concerned, little perception was required to come to the conclusion that subscription income to the Scott Memorial Appeal had fallen far short of expectations.

John Smith, Clockmakers of Derby, were engaged to produce a clock for the Tower, the design for which was agreed upon at a meeting of the City's Parks and Open Spaces Committee in March 1914.[191] It was agreed that the Clock Tower, in the form of a lighthouse, should be sited at the south end of Roath Park lake in front of the embankment where the figurehead of the *Terra Nova* had been placed. The construction of the Tower itself was carried out by workmen and officials of the Cardiff City Council under the direction of the City Engineer, William Harpur, and was completed by January 1915,[192] at a cost of £159.6s.8d. in wages and materials.[193] More than three years after its completion, on Monday, 14 October 1918, less than a month before the end of the First World War and more than six years since Scott and his companions had lost their lives in the Antarctic, the Clock Tower was officially presented to the City of Cardiff by its donor, Mr. F.C. Bowring.[194]

Since that time, and effectively since 1915, the Clock Tower, dedicated to Capt. Scott and his brave companions, has stood as a familiar sight to all who visit Roath Park lake and as such has served as the principal and most prominent monument to the unique connexion between Cardiff and the British Antarctic Expedition (1910).

NOTES

[1] Roland Huntford, *Scott and Amundsen*, (1979). For comment see especially, Wayland Young, 'On the Debunking of Captain Scott: a critique against Myths, Errors and Distortions', *Encounter* (May, 1980), 8–19; 'Scott and Amundsen: an exchange between Roland Huntford and Wayland Young', *ibid.* (Nov., 1980), 85–89.

[2] Huntford, *Scott and Amundsen*, p. 269, says Evans went to see Markham in May 1909.

[3] Lord Mountevans, *Adventurous Life* (1946), p. 80.

[4] *ibid.*, p. 247.

[5] *Who's Who 1933*; *Who's Who in Wales 1937*.

[6] This and what follows is based upon the account written by W.E. Davies, *Western Mail*, (hereafter *WM*) 28 June 1913, 'Wales and the South Pole: An Undisclosed Fact. The 1910 Expedition might have been all Welsh'. Davies wrote that he received his 'phone call from Griffiths 'almost exactly four years ago'.

[7] *45th Annual Report of the Incorporated Cardiff Chamber of Commerce, 1910.*

[8] Scott Polar Research Institute, Cambridge (hereafter SPRI) MS 715/9 f. 4, 'Diary of Sir Clements Markham'.

[9] *ibid.*; Sir Clements Markham, 'Robert Falcon Scott', *Cornhill Magazine*, (Apr. 1913), 462.

[10] Markham, in his 'Diary', SPRI MS 715/9, says that Scott and Evans met on 9 July 1909 (Friday), the day which he repeats in his article in the *Cornhill Magazine* (Apr. 1913). W.E. Davies, however, who was intimately involved in the negotiations between the two men, in his article *WM*, 28 June 1913, refers directly to Markham's article in the *Cornhill Magazine*, where he says Sir Clements 'has made a slight mistake in the chronological sequence of events', and insists that the meeting between Scott and Evans in fact took place on 16 July—the following Friday.

[11] Here it has been argued that Evans, on his own initiative and quite independently, had canvassed for support from Cardiff for his proposed Expedition and that this aspect of his preparations had reached a fairly advanced stage by the time of his meeting with Scott on 16 July 1909. Evans, himself, in the course of several published works scarcely refers to his preparations to mount his own Antarctic Expedition, and certainly makes no specific reference to Cardiff. The nearest he came was in one vague remark made nearly forty years after the event when, as Admiral Lord Mountevans, he wrote in *Adventurous Life*, (1946) '1909 saw me planning to fit out and lead another Antarctic Expedition . . . I found many supporters in Wales . . . '

[12] W.E. Davies, *WM*, 28 June 1913.

[13] Huntford, *Scott and Amundsen*, p. 305.

[14] *WM*, 16, 18, 20 Sept. 1909.

[15] *ibid.*, 13 Oct. 1909.

[16] *ibid.*, 26 Oct. 1909.

[17] *ibid.*, 17 June 1913. Evans acknowledged the help he had received from W.E. Davies and the staff of the *Western Mail* in getting to know those who had money.

[18] *WM*, 1 Nov. 1909; *South Wales Daily News*, (hereafter *SWDN*) 1 Nov. 1909, says £330.10s.0d. subscribed.

[19] *WM*, 2 November 1909; 17 June 1913.

[20] R. Pound, *Evans of the Broke*, (Oxford, 1965), p. 55.

[21] J. Geraint Jenkins, *Evan Thomas Radcliffe: a Cardiff Shipping Company*, (National Museum of Wales, 1982), pp. 15–16, 40–41.

[22] *W.M.*, 2 Nov. 1909.

[23] Stephen J. Gwynn, *Captain Scott*, (1929), p. 158, quoting a letter from Scott, 25 November 1909, R.F. Scott, *Scott's Last Expedition*, (arranged Leonard Huxley) 2 vols. (1913), II, 499.

[24] Pound, *Evans of the Broke*, p. 60 and Huntford, *Scott and Amundsen*, p. 284.

[25] *WM*, 24 Nov. 1909.

[26] This is implicit in Scott's private notes of 25 November 1909, for example, Gwynn, *Capt. Scott*, p. 158.

[27] *WM*, 30 November and 1 Dec. 1909.

[28] *ibid.*, 30 November and 2 Dec. 1909.

[29] *ibid.*, 2 Dec. 1909.

[30] *ibid.*, 7 Jan. 1910, for the General Election of 1910, Neal Blewett, *The Peers, the parties and the People, the General Election of 1910*, (1972).

[31] *WM*, 7 Jan. 1910, and Huntford, *Scott and Amundsen*, p. 270; David Thomson, *Scott's Men*, (1977), p. 159.

[32] *Times*, 18 March 1935 (Obituary notice of W.E. Davies); *WM*, 22 Aug. 1957 (Obituary notice of Lt. Evans, then Lord Mountevans).

[33] *WM*, 28 June 1913; 30 Nov. 1948 (Obituary notice of John Rowland); *Who was Who, 1941–1950* (sub John Rowland).

[34] *WM*, 26 Feb. 1910.

[35] Huntford, *Scott and Amundsen*, p. 271 and *The Worst Journey in the World*, (Penguin ed., edited by George Seaver, 1970), p. 11.

[35a] Glamorgan Record Office, Cardiff (hereafter Glam. R.O.) D/D Com. C. General Minute Book of the Cardiff Incorporated Shippers Assoc., 1903–10, p. 669; *WM*, 11 June 1910, reports that Alderman Chappell was unable to attend the meetings of the Trimming Board on Wed. 8 June because of the arrival of the *Terra Nova*. See also *SWDN*, 17 June 1910. For a history of the Coal Trimmers' Union, see Martin Daunton, 'The Cardiff Coal Trimmers' Union, 1888–1914', *Llafur*, 2 (1976), 10–24.

[36] *45th Annual Report of the Cardiff Incorporated Chamber of Commerce, 1910*; *WM*, 30 May 1910.

[37] Cardiff City Records, City Hall, Cardiff (hereafter Cardiff CR) Box 1584, Evans to Chappell, 19 Apr. 1910, from the offices of the British Antarctic Expedition (1910), 36 & 38 Victoria St., London S.W.

[38] *ibid.*, 2 May 1910.

[39] *ibid.*, Scott to Chappell, 5 May 1910, from the offices of the British Antarctic Expedition (1910).

[40] E.R.G.R. Evans, *South with Scott*, (1921), p. 15.

[41] 'Luncheon to the British Antarctic Expedition, 1910', *Geographical Journal*, XXXVI (July 1910), 11–26.

[42] *WM*, 10 June 1910.

[43] SPRI MS 852/12 Diary of P.O. Keohane.

[44] *WM*, 10 June 1910.

[45] SPRI MS 870 Diary of P.O. Frank Browning, 1 June 1910–30 Dec. 1911.

[46] *ibid.*

[47] *WM*, 7 June 1910; Cardiff CR, Box 1584, invitations from Alderman Chappell to join the welcoming party were distributed by the Town Clerk of Cardiff, J.L. Wheatley, 9 June 1910.

[48] SPRI MS 208/12/1 Log of the *Terra Nova*; Vol. I, *ibid.*, MS 825/2, Log of P.O. Keohane.

[49] *WM*, 10 June 1910; *SWDN*, 10 June 1910.

[50] Cardiff CR, Box 1270, Menu and invitations; *WM*, 7 Dec. 1904. This was at the old Town Hall, St. Mary Street, Cardiff.

[51] *WM*, 10 June 1910.

[52] *ibid.*, 11 June 1910.

[53] SPRI MS 280/12/1 Log of the *Terra Nova*, Vol. I, 10 June 1910.

[54] *WM*, 11 June 1910; *SWDN*, 11 June 1910.

[55] *ibid.*, 13 June 1910.

[56] *ibid.*

[57] SPRI MS 280/28/41.

[58] *ibid.* MS 280/12/1, Log of the *Terra Nova*, Vol. I.

[59] *WM*, 11 June 1910; Cardiff CR, Box 1584, Invitation by Herbert J. Taylor of Moss's Empires to the Lord Mayor for the ship's company, 8 June 1910.

[60] *ibid.*, 13 June 1910; Evans, *South with Scott*, p. 13: SPRI MS 870 Diary of Frank Browning and MS 280/12/1, Log of the *Terra Nova*, Vol. I, 11 June 1910, records a total of 406.15 tons of coal aboard.

[61] Royal Institution, Swansea, a post card of P.O. Edgar Evans, 21 June 1910, mentions seeing Sarah in Cardiff before the *Terra Nova* departed. *WM*, 12 Feb. 1913, printed a photograph of June 1910 of Edgar Evans and his wife Lois and one child aboard the *Terra Nova* in Cardiff Docks.

During the 1960s, Stanley Richards, the curator of the Swansea Museum, worked strenuously, but unsuccessfully, to try to achieve fitting recognition for Edgar Evans in Swansea. Recent years, however, have witnessed a revival of interest in Evans. As a result of an initiative by the Cardiff-based Capt. Scott Society, at a civic ceremony in the Brangwyn Hall, Swansea, on 17 Feb. 1994 there was unveiled a bust of Edgar Evans sculpted by Philip Chatfield. Recent writings on Evans have included G.C. Gregor's pamphlet, *Edgar Evans: Antarctic Explorer* (Swansea Museum, 1993), and his book, *Swansea's Antarctic Explorer: Edgar Evans, 1876-1912*, (Swansea, 1995).

[62] Cardiff CR, MS Box 1584, invitation of the manager, 7 June 1910; *WM*, 13 June 1910.

[63] SPRI MS 280/28/3 British Antarctic Expedition (1910), Statement of Accounts; *SWDN*, 13 June 1910.

[64] *ibid.* MS 870. Diary of P.O. Frank Browning.

[65] Cardiff CR, MS Box 1584. Letter from Gethin Lewis to the Lord Mayor, 8 June 1910.

[66] *WM*, 2 June 1910; R.F. Scott, *Scott's Last Expedition* (arranged by Leonard Huxley), II, 494.

[67] *WM*, 15 June 1910; Cardiff CR, MS Box 1584. Letter from the Treasurer, Mr. A.B. Badger, of the League of Empire, Monmouthshire Branch, Newport, in which he informs Lord Mayor John Chappell that the cost of the aneroid barometers was met from a balance of receipts of a lecture by Sir Ernest Shackleton.

[68] *WM*, 14 June 1910.

[69] SPRI MS 280/28/4d. British Antarctic Expedition, 1910-13, vol. 14, 'Terra Nova'. Engineer's stores correspondence.

[70] *Scott's Last Expedition* (arranged by Huxley), I, 623.

[71] Huntford, *Scott and Amundsen*, pp. 330-34. *WM*, 16 June carries a picture of

seaman displaying for sightseers two esquimaux dogs.

[72] *WM*, 15 June 1910.

[73] *SWDN*, 15 June 1910.

[74] SPRI MS 852/2. Log of P.O. Keohane.

[75] *South Wales Echo*, 14 Feb. 1972.

[76] *South with Scott*, p. 3.

[77] *WM*, 14 June 1910.

[78] This account of the arrangements for the dinner is based on the minutes of the Cardiff Chamber of Commerce 1907-10, p. 404 in Glam. R.O. MS D/D Com/C; see also *WM*, 8 and 9 June 1910.

[78] The Alexandra Room was re-named the Scott Room in 1982. Attached to the chimney breast is a small plaque commemorating the event: 'In this room, on Monday, June 13th 1910, Captain Robert Falcon Scott, R.N., attended his last public banquet before sailing from Cardiff on the Terra Nova on his last voyage to the Antarctic'. It appears that the original plaque had been lost, and, on the initiative of Mr David Maxwell, a Director of the brewers Ind Coope and Allsopp, at a celebratory dinner on 7 Dec. 1953 there was unveiled the plaque currently on display in the Scott Room. *WM*, 7, 8 Dec. 1953. The existence of a copy of the original menu came to public attention as recently as 1982 when a relative of a guest at the dinner drew attention to its existence, on the basis of which was held, on 13 June 1982, a recreation of the menu of 13 June 1910. *South Wales Echo* 23 Feb., 11 June 1982, *WM*, 17 May 1982.

[80] The following account of the proceedings at the dinner on 13 June 1910 is based on the report of the event in the *WM*, 14 June 1910.

[81] *ibid.*, 17 June 1913.

[82] *ibid.*, 15 June 1910.

[83] SPRI MS 715/9. Notebook of Sir Clements Markham.

[84] *ibid.*, MS 870. Diary of Frank Browning.

[85] Cardiff CR, Box 1584. Guest list for the civic reception. A note at the foot of the list says 798 (guests). The names of those who attended were printed in *WM*, 15 June 1910.

[86] *WM*, 15 June 1910.

[87] Royal Institution, Swansea. Copy of a letter by the Director, Stanley Richards, to the author R. Pound, 18 June 1965, concerning his conversation with Sarah, Mrs. Owen, Sketty, Swansea, who recalled Evans's condition following the reception.

[88] Stephen Gwynn, *Capt. Scott* (1920), p. 204.

[89] SPRI MS 715/9. Notebook of Sir Clements Markham; *ibid.* MS 852/2, P.O. Keohane 'Log' of the Terra Nova. Schermuley was present at the civic reception of 14 June, *WM*, 15 June 1910: *SWDN*, 16 June 1910 reported that one of the crew was paid off on Monday evening.

[90] *WM*, 16 June 1910; *SWDN*, 18 June 1910.

[90a] Sue Limb and Patrick Cordingley, *Captain Oates, Soldier and Explorer* (1982), p. 97.

[91] Royal Institution, Swansea. Copy of a letter from Stanley Richards to Reginald Pound, 14 June 1965, in which he conveys the reminiscences of Sarah (Mrs. Owen), who accompanied her uncle to Scott's cabin.

[92] *WM*, 16 June 1910. Except where otherwise stated this description of the departure of the *Terra Nova* is based on this report.

[93] Edward Wilson, *Diary of the Terra Nova Expedition to the Antarctic 1910-12* (ed. H.G.R. King, (1972), p. 12.

[94] Glam. R.O. MS D/D Com/C, Minute Book of the Cardiff Chamber of Commerce, 1907-10, p. 404; *SWDN*, 9 June 1910; Cardiff CR Box 1581, Secretary of Bristol Channel Passenger Boats 'Red Funnel Line', 13 June 1910, sends a supply of invitation cards to members of the City Council to join a steamer to witness the departure of the *Terra Nova.*

[95] *South with Scott*, p13.

[96] *WM,* 17 June 1913.

[97] *ipid.,* 14 June 1910.

[98] *SWDN,* 16 June 1910, p. 4.

[99] *WM,* 16 June 1910. A personal letter from Scott to Chappell dated 17 June 1910 was published in *SWDN,* 12 Feb. 1913.

Mr Dear Lord Mayor,

I am sending you a photograph, which I hope you will accept, with renewed thanks for the great personal kindness and hospitality with which you entertained me in Cardiff. The memory of the visit will long be with me.

Yours very sincerely,

R. Scott

P.S. I trust news will improve from Canada. [Chappell had confided to Scott of difficulties faced by his son in Canada.]

[100] *ibid.,* 17 June 1910.

[101] *ibid.,* 11 Feb. 1913.

[102] *ibid.,* 17 June 1913; Evans made a special mention of Radcliffe's unique contribution to the Expedition in an appendix to *Scott's Last Expedition* (arranged by Leonard Huxley), II, 499.

[103] SPRI MS 286/28/2. Under two months before the *Terra Nova* was due to sail £14,000 had been subscribed.

[104] *ibid.* MS 238/2. P.O. Keohane's Diary; *WM,* 12 Feb. 1913; *SWDN,* 11 Feb. 1913.

[105] Cardiff Central Library MS 3.781, 'Terra Nova Expedition' correspondence, Lt. Evans to Daniel Radcliffe, Madeira, 26 June 1910.

[106] *ibid.,* Lt. Evans to Daniel Radcliffe, 'at sea 1500 miles from Simonstown', 6 Aug. 1910. This letter and other items from this correspondence were utilised by Dan O'Neil, 'Off to the Pole–with a city's cheers behind them', *South Wales Echo,* 28 June 1982.

[107] Pound, *Evans of the Broke,* pp. 60-62.

[108] Cardiff Central Library MS 3.781. Lt. H. Rennick to Daniel Radcliffe, Aug. 1910 'at sea Madeira to Simonstown'.

[109] H. Ludlam, *Capt. Scott: the Full Story,* (1965), pp. 148-9.

[110] *SWDN,* 17 Feb. 1913, published Scott's letter of 28 Aug. 1910.

[111] Minutes of the Cardiff City Property and Markets Committee, 9 Sept. 1910.

[112] Huxley, *Scott of the Antarctic,* p. 197.

[113] Cardiff Central Library MS 3.781. Lt. Evans to Daniel Radcliffe, 2 Oct. 1910.

[104] SPRI MS 280/28/2. H.L.L. Pennell, handwritten report of the British Antarctic Expedition, 1910-13, vol. 4 'Terra Nova'. Typescript of the report is SPRI MS 280/28/4a.

[115] Garrard, *The Worst Journey in the World*, p. 68; Huntford, *Scott and Amundsen*, p. 331.

[116] SPRI MS 280/28/2, Pennell's Report; Evans. *South with Scott*, p. 13.

[117] Garrard, *The World Journey in the World*, p. 88.

[118] *SWDN*, 12 Feb 1913, published the text of the card which was wrongly ascribed to Dec. 1910.

[119] Garrard, *The Worst Journey in the World*, pp. 88-9.

[120] Huntford, *Scott and Amundsen*, p. 330.

[121] *ibid.*, and Garrard, *The Worst Journey in the World*, p. 100.

[122] Cardiff Central Library MS 3.781 Lt. Evans to Daniel Radcliffe, 1 Jan. 1911.

[123] Garrard, *The Worst Journey in the World*, p. 160; Huntford, *Scott and Amundsen*, p. 366.

[124] A.R. Ellis, (ed.) *Under Scott's Command: Lashly's Antarctic Diaries*, (1969), pp. 105, 108.

[125] Cardiff Central Library MS 3.781, Capt. Scott to Daniel Radcliffe, Feb. 1911.

[126] *ibid.*, Lt. Evans to Daniel Radcliffe, Cape Evans, 3 a.m . 7 Sept, 1911.

[127] Pound, *Evans of the Broke*, p. 87-8; Cherry Garrard in his *Worst Journeys in the World*, pp. 74-5, 363, also extols the virtue of Crown Patent Fuel. See also *South Wales Echo*, 16 Mar. 1961, for photograph of Cardiff Patent Fuel on a sledge at Cape Evans, 1910.

[128] *WM*, 11 Feb. 1913.

[129] The best account of these events is *The Diary of William Lashly: a Record of the Return Journey of the Supporting Party with Captain Scott to the South Pole* (with a foreword by Sir Edward R.G. Evans privately printed, University of Reading, 1938-9). See also W. Lashly, 'A Story of the White Wastes. My last journey with Capt. Scott'. *Powell Duffryn Review*, no. 104 (Oct. 1955). [Lashly, a Hampshire man, upon his return from the Antarctic was offered a job with the Board of Trade in Cardiff which he took up at the end of the First World War. He lived at 17 Mayfield Avenue until his return to Hampshire in 1932.]

[130] *WM*, 27 June 1912; Pound, *Evans of the Broke*, p. 121.

[131] *WM*, 11 Feb. 1913.

[132] *ibid.*, 4 Dec. 1912.

[133] SPRI MS 280/12/2 'Log of the Terra Nova', vol. II, 18 Jan. 1913.

[134] Cardiff Central Library MS 3.781. Letters of Daniel Radcliffe to Capt. Scott from Cardiff 21 Oct. 1911 and Drake's reply, 25 Jan. 1913. McMurdo Sound.

[135] Pound, *Evans of the Broke*, p. 24.

[136] *WM*, 13 Feb. 1913, published a photograph; *SWDN*, 11 Feb, 1913. The painting by Cardiff artist Capt. Richard Short was commissioned after the *Terra Nova* left Cardiff in June 1910 as a result of a subscription organised in the Docks community by Alderman W.H. Renwick and Mr. W.H. Newton, *The South Wales Echo* 15 July 1968 reported that Short's painting was to be sold in London. At the sale at Coe's–later Christie's–owing to the efforts of Mr. Peter Philp, the Cardiff antique dealer, the painting was purchased for a private collection in South Wales. I am much indebted to Mr. Philp for having provided detailed information about this purchase. For two articles on Short by Peter Philp see, 'Richard Short: Master Mariner and Master Painter', *Antique Finder*, Vol.13 No.7 (July 1974) and *WM* 15 June 1974.

[137] *WM*, 12 Feb. 1913.

[138] *ibid.*, 17 Feb. 1913.

[139] Cardiff CR, Box 1732, Sir Edgar Speyer to Radcliffe, 20 Feb. 1913, 7 Lothbury, E.C. The epilogue in *Scott's Last Expedition* (arr. Huxley) pays tribute to the work of the British Antarctic Committee, including Daniel Radcliffe, 'who was invited to join at Commander Evans' request.' In fact, as described, Radcliffe was not appointed to the Committee of the British Antarctic Expedition (1910) until he was co-opted in 1913.

[140] *ibid.*, Box 1851.

[141] *ibid.*, Box 1732.

[142] *ibid.*, Box 1851, 5 Mar. 1913.

[143] *ibid.*

[144] *WM*, 22 Apr. 1913; Evans was created K.C.B. 6 May 1913, Pound, *Evans of the Broke*, p. 126.

[145] *WM*, 23 Apr. 1913.

[146] *ibid.*, 5 May 1913; *Cambrian Daily Leader*, 5 May 1913. For a recent biography of Kathleen Scott, see Louisa Young, *A Great Task of Happiness; The Life of Kathleen Scott*, (1995).

[147] *WM*, 11, 12, 13 June 1913.

[148] *South Wales Argus*, 13 June 1913; *WM*, 14 June 1913; *Times*, 16 June 1913.

[149] *WM*, 14 June 1913.

[150] *ibid.*, 16 June 1913.

[151] *Times*, 16 June 1913. Peter Scott was 3 years and 4 months old on the occasion of his visit to Cardiff. As far as he can recall the highlight of his visit to the *Terra Nova* was to be taken up to the crows nest by P.O. Tom Crean. I am indebted to Sir Peter Scott for this reminiscence.

[152] *WM*, 16 June 1913.

[153] *ibid.*, 17 June 1913.

[154] Cardiff Central Library MS 3.781, G. Murray Levick to Daniel Radcliffe, Buxted, Sussex, 21 June 1913.

[155] *WM*, 26 June 1913.

[156] *ibid.*, 28 June 1913. 'Wales and the South Pole: an undisclosed fact. The 1910 Expedition might have been all Welsh'.

[157] *ibid.*, 1 July 1913. Article by the 'Vicar of Aberpergwm', J.Ll. Thomas.

[158] *ibid.*, 2 July 1913; *Cardiff Naturalists' Society: Report and Transactions*, XLII (1914), 134.

[159] Evans, *Adventurous Life*, pp. 83–4; Pound, *Evans of the Broke*, p. 131.

[160] *WM*, 1 & 7 July 1913; *SWDN*, 2 July 1913.

[161] Minutes of the Cardiff Parks and Open Spaces Committee, 16 July & 26 Nov. 1913.

[162] *WM*, 7 July, 15, 16 Aug. 1913; *SWDN*. 16 Aug. 1913 carries four photographs of the departure of the *Terra Nova*.

[163] Cardiff CR, Box 1732, receipt signed by Daniel Radcliffe acknowledging the cheque by Lord Merthyr on behalf of the Cardiff Railway Co., 27 Nov. 1913.

[164] *WM*, 9 Dec. 1913. The figurehead of the *Terra Nova* now resides in the National Museum of Wales, Cardiff.

The *Terra Nova* returned briefly to Cardiff in 1916 to deliver a cargo of pit-props. She continued working in and around Newfoundland until she was sunk on 13 Sept. 1943, following the failure of her auxiliary engine and having caught fire, while carrying supplies between Newfoundland and American bases in Greenland. Her 24 man crew was rescued by the Coastguard cutter USS *Atak* after which she attempted to sink *Terra Nova* to ensure that she posed no danger to shipping. The actual sinking at Lat. 61 08N, 45 25W, was effected by shells fired by the larger and more heavily armed support vessel, the ocean-going tug USS *Laurel*. For information about the sinking of the *Terra Nova* I owe my thanks to Mr. Malcolm Marsden of the Cardiff-based Capt. Scott Society.

As a means of promoting the close links between Cardiff and the British Antarctic Expedition (1910), a 'Terra Nova Trust' was established by the Capt. Scott Society on 13 June 1994 with the aim of raising sufficient funds to build a working replica of the Expedition ship, incorporating the most modern technology and equipment, to be based at the proposed Scott Harbour at Cardiff Bay.

[165] *ibid.* Evans pointed out that because of Cardiff 'and the influence of Welsh friends'–especially the government grant of £20000–South Wales produced £24000, or some 60 per cent of the subscription income required for the UK to mount the 1910 Expedition.

In an article, *WM* 2 May 1919, 'The British Expedition to the South Pole. How the "Western Mail" helped Captain Scott', written in celebration of the 25th anniversary of the *Western Mail*, Evans adjusted this figure upwards to £26000. I owe this latter reference to Michael Tarver. I am indebted to Commander Evans's grandson, the 3rd Baron Mountevans, for his observation, in a letter, on the significance of Cardiff in funding the British Antarctic Expedition (1910). 'Family wisdom has it that without such support the expedition simply would not have sailed'.

[166] *MW,* 9 Dec. 1913.

[167] For Cardiff politics in this period, see M.J. Daunton, *Coal Metropolis: Cardiff 1870-1914* (Leicester U.P., 1977), especially chapter 9.

[168] The letter from Ald. Morgan Thomas, Daniel Radcliffe and J.L. Wheatley, 3 Dec. 1914, makes this clear, see note 177.

[169] Cardiff CR. Box 1851. Letter from J.L. Wheatley to Lady Scott, 28 June 1914.

[170] *ibid.,* copy of letter from J.L. Wheatley to Commander Evans, 24 June 1914, and reply from Commander Evans to Wheatley, 'Quamby', Ford Road, Stokes Bay.

[171] *ibid.,* Lady Scott to J.L. Wheatley, 29 June 1914, 174 Buckingham Palace Road, London S.W.

[172] *ibid.,* 6 July 1914.

[173] *ibid.,* Miss G.M. Scott to J.L. Wheatley, 21 Oct. 1914, from 4 Cheyne Court, London S.W.

[174] *ibid.,* Wheatley to Radcliffe, 24 Nov. 1914, at Evan Thomas and Radcliffe, 4 Dock Chambers.

[175] *ibid.*

[176] *ibid.,* Radcliffe to Wheatley, 25 Nov. 1914.

[177] *ibid.,* letter from Ald. Morgan Thomas, Daniel Radcliffe and J.L. Wheatley to the Property and Markets Committee, 3 Dec. 1914; and proceedings of the Committee, 21 Dec. 1914.

[178] *ibid.,* Lady Scott to Wheatley, 2 Feb. 1915, as from 174 Buckingham Palace Road, London S.W.

[179] *ibid.,* received by Wheatley, 11 Feb. 1915.

[180] *ibid.,* Mrs. Brownlow to Wheatley, 26 Mar. 1915, from Shirley, Henley-on-Thames. Wheatley to Mrs Brownlow, 29 Mar. 1915.

[181] *ibid.,* W.W. Wagstaffe, 2 Justice Studios, Justice Walk, Chelsea, London S.W.,

to Wheatley, 23 June 1915; Wheatley to Wagstaffe, 24 June 1915.

[182] *ibid.,* Wagstaffe to Wheatley, 5 Feb. 1916.

[183] *ibid.,* Wagstaffe to Wheatley, 20 Nov. 1915.

[184] *ibid.,* Alexander Parlanti, Artistic Foundry, to Wheatley, 28 Oct. 1915.

[185] *ibid.,* Wheatley to Wagstaffe, 3 Feb. 1916.

[186] *ibid.,* Radcliffe to Wheatley, 9 Mar. 1916.

[187] *ibid.,* Wheatley to Major-General Sir Francis Lloyd, Major General Commanding London District, Whitehall, S.W., 10 Mar. 1916.

[188] *ibid.,* Lt. Lisburne, ADC to Major General Sir Francis Lloyd, to Wheatley, 30 Mar. 1916; Wheatley to Lt. Lisburne, 31 Mar. 1916.

[189] *ibid.,* Radcliffe to Wheatley, 1 Apr. 1916.

[190] *WM,* 11 Apr. 1916. These two plaques, together with all other memorial plaques erected at the Royal Hamadryad Hospital, were removed from the Hospital during a period of reorganisation in the 1970s. I am much indebted to Mrs. Sheila Rees, Hospital Administrator, for her interest in locating the whereabouts of the plaques in store. In 1917 Mr. & Mrs. Percy Miles of Ty-Gwyn Road, Penylan, endowed a plaque to the memory of Lt. H.L.L. Pennell, R.N., navigating officer of the *Terra Nova* who went down with his ship HMS *Queen Mary* at the Battle of Jutland, in 1916. In 1918, Daniel Radcliffe endowed another bed 'In Memory of the Brave Deeds of Captain Evans both on 'Terra Nova' and on HMS 'Broke'. Lt. Evans in fact, lived until 1957.

[191] Minutes of the Parks and Open Spaces Committee, 12 Mar. 1914.

[192] *ibid.,* 7 Jan. 1915.

[193] Cardiff CR., Box 1947, Report of the City Treasurer and Controller, 3 Feb. 1915, to the Chairman and Members of the Parks Committee.

[194] *WM,* 15 Oct. 1918.